EDITED BY DAVID SIMON

T0341349

RETHINKING SUSTAINABLE CITIES

Accessible, green and fair

POLICY PRESS SHORTS POLICY & PRACTICE

First published in Great Britain in 2016 by

Policy Press
University of Bristol
1-9 Old Park Hill
Bristol
BS2 8BB
UK
+44 (0)117 954 5940
pp-info@bristol.ac.uk
www.policypress.co.uk

North America office:
Policy Press
c/o The University of Chicago Press
1427 East 60th Street
Chicago, IL 60637, USA
t: +1 773 702 7700
f: +1 773 702 9756
sales@press.uchicago.edu
www.press.uchicago.edu

British Library Cataloguing in Publication Data
A catalogue record for this book is available from the British Library.

Library of Congress Cataloging-in-Publication Data
A catalog record for this book has been requested.

ISBN 978-1-4473-3284-8 (paperback)
ISBN 978-1-4473-3287-9 (ePub)
ISBN 978-1-4473-3286-2 (Mobi)

Cover design by Policy Press
Front cover: Partial view of Bangkok. Photo copyright David Simon
Printed and bound by CPI Group (UK) Ltd, Croydon, CR0 4YY
Policy Press uses environmentally responsible print partners

Contents

List of plates   iv

List of tables and figures   vi

Acronyms and abbreviations   vii

About the authors   ix

Acknowledgements   xi

Foreword   xiii

Julio D Dávila

1   Introduction: sustainable cities in sustainable societies   1

    David Simon

2   Accessible cities: from urban density to multidimensional accessibility   11

    James Waters

3   Green cities: from tokenism to incrementalism and transformation   61

    David Simon

4   Fair cities: imperatives in meeting global sustainable developmental aspirations   107

    Susan Parnell

5   Conclusions, implications and practical guidelines   145

    Henrietta Palmer and David Simon

Selected relevant internet resources   167

Index   175

List of plates

2.1 Manhattan borough in New York City (USA), parts of Tokyo (Japan), Singapore   14
and Hong Kong (pictured) have some of the highest residential densities in formal
housing in the world by virtue of numerous high rise apartment blocks. These cater
for a range of income categories, right up to the elite, with social amenities also in
close proximity (Photo © David Simon)

2.2 The highest residential densities in informal housing are found in many   15
shantytowns and so-called slums in large cities in the global South. Rio de Janeiro,
Brazil, (pictured) is distinctive in terms of the close juxtaposition of high density
favelas and middle income apartments (Photo © David Simon)

2.3 The lowest residential densities are found in high income suburbs worldwide,   15
characterised by large double-storey mansions or single story bungalow/villa houses
on extensive plots. Middle-class housing, as here in Ensenada, Mexico, generally
occupies smaller plots but densities are still comparatively low (Photo © David
Simon)

2.4 The trade-offs among different forms of accessibility are well illustrated by   30
these informal traders in central Lagos, Nigeria, who locate themselves to maximise
passing trade, despite the noise and apparent inconvenience of their stall's site
(Photo © David Simon)

2.5 This minibus terminus in Dakar, Senegal, is a key accessibility hub for this part   36
of the metropolis, linking diverse areas with affordable motor transport (Photo ©
David Simon)

2.6 Pedestrianised streets in high density commercial areas like Chinatown in   39
Singapore, maximise accessibility and shopper densities, while increasing pollution-
free amenity (Photo © David Simon)

3.1 Classic urban greening – 'the city beautiful' – in downtown Vancouver,   68
Canada (Photo © David Simon)

3.2 The humid tropics facilitate natural urban greenness, although often blended   68
with well-maintained gardens, as here in a hillside high income area of Kampala,
Uganda (Photo © David Simon)

3.3 Even in the humid tropics, high density, low income areas often lack the   69
greenery of high income areas, with exposed brown earth reflecting a lack of
investment and maintained public spaces, and sometimes also livestock grazing
pressure. The multi-purpose value of trees, like this one planted as part of an action
research project in peri-urban Kumasi, Ghana, is therefore high (Photo © David
Simon)

3.4 Intensive peri-urban agriculture, Lagos, Nigeria (Photo © David Simon)   71

3.5 Conservation of ground cover on steep slopes and of some vegetation in and   82
around informal settlements maintains slope stability, intercepts storm run-off and
improves soil penetration by rainwater. These valuable ecosystem services are vital
for poor and wealthy alike, as here in peri-urban Durban, South Africa, in the context
of extreme events and climate change (Photo © David Simon)

3.6 Green walls and balcony or roof gardens, as here in Manhattan,   87
New York City (USA), are aesthetically attractive and important for carbon
sequestration (Photo © David Simon)

3.7 Green infrastructure: the Hudson River Park on Manhattan's Lower West Side,   88
which replaced derelict wharves and warehouses, has provided valuable green shade
and recreation space, and increased urban biodiversity and carbon sequestration
capacity (Photo © David Simon)

3.8 Nanjing (People's Republic of China) exemplifies urban infrastructural   89
greening as part of comprehensive redevelopment to tackle industrial pollution and
unsustainable urbanism (Photos © David Simon)

4.1 Different life prospects: City traders, London; second-hand clothing vendor   109
and customers, Maputo; beggar, Copenhagen, respectively (London and Copenhagen
© Susan Parnell; Maputo © David Simon)

List of tables and figures

Tables

3.1 Comparison of the green and brown agendas with respect to urban solid   70
waste management. Source: modified after Allen et al, 2002, Figure 2.3, p 36.

Figures

3.1 Schematic representation of relationships between urban greening and   85
human physical activity levels. Source: Modified after Trundle and McEvoy,
2016, Figure 19.3, p 281.

Acronyms and abbreviations

BREEAM	Building Research Establishment Environmental Assessment Methodology (UK)
BRICS	Brazil, Russia, India, China and South Africa grouping of countries
CBA	community-based adaptation
CCCI	Cities and Climate Change Initiative
COP21	Twenty-first Conference of the Parties to the UNFCCC
DRR	disaster risk reduction
EbA	ecosystem-based adaptation
GBCSA	Green Building Council of South Africa
Habitat III	third 20-yearly global summit on urbanisation and human settlements, Quito, October 2016
ICLEI	Local Governments for Sustainability
ICT	information and communication technologies
IIED	International Institute of Environment and Development
IPCC	Intergovernmental Panel on Climate Change
MDGs	Millennium Development Goals
MOSS	Metropolitan Open Space System
MUF	Mistra Urban Futures
NGO	non-governmental organisation
OECD	Organization for Economic Co-operation and Development

PES	payment for ecosystem services
PV	photovoltaic
SDG	Sustainable Development Goals
SUD–NET	Sustainable Urban Development Network
TCPA	Town and Country Planning Association (UK)
TOD	transit-oriented development
UCLG	United Cities and Local Governments
UNEP	United Nations Environment Programme
UNFCCC	United Nations Framework Convention on Climate Change
UN–HABITAT	United Nations Human Settlements Programme
UPA	urban and peri-urban agriculture
WCED	World Commission on Environment and Development

About the authors

David Simon is Director of Mistra Urban Futures, Chalmers University, Gothenburg, and Professor of Development Geography at Royal Holloway, University of London. He specialises in development–environment issues, with particular reference to cities, climate change and sustainability, and the relationships between theory, policy and practice, on all of which he has published extensively. He is author of *Cities, Capital and Development*, editor of *Fifty Key Thinkers on Development*, and has co-edited several recent books on different development–environment challenges and within the last year, special issues of *Urban Climate* and of *Current Opinion on Environmental Sustainability* on urban climate adaptation. His extensive research experience spans sub-Saharan Africa, tropical Asia, the UK, the USA and Sweden.

Henrietta Palmer is an architect and Professor of Urban Design at Chalmers University in Gothenburg. She is also Deputy Scientific Director at Mistra Urban Futures, Gothenburg. Henrietta previously held a position as Professor of Architecture at the Royal Institute of Art, Stockholm, where, during a ten year period, she developed the post-masters programme, *Resources*, as an interdisciplinary research space on the challenges of our urban futures, with a particular focus on the cities of the global South. Her current research focuses on the urban transformation processes and the visual language of change.

Recently she published *Access to Resources: An Urban Agenda*, which she initiated and edited.

Susan Parnell is Professor of Urban Geography and co-founder of the African Centre for Cities at the University of Cape Town. She has held previous academic positions at Wits University and the School of Oriental and African Studies as well as visiting research fellowships from LSE, Oxford, Durham and the British Academy. She was a Leverhulme Visiting Professor at UCL and revised this chapter for publication while Emeka Anyaoku Visiting Chair, University of London. Recent co-edited books include *Climate at a City Scale*; *The Routledge Handbook on Cities of the Global South* and *Africa's Urban Revolution*.

James Waters is an interdisciplinary researcher and consultant at Arup International Development. He co-founded the Urban Resilience Research Network (URNET) and has written articles on dimensions of urban resilience, migration and the urban poor. His PhD focused on the resilience of slum-dwellers in Kampala, Uganda, assessing the role of ecosystem services and determinants of adaptive capacity. He is currently working on projects around urban risk in Africa and using network analysis to understand complex urban systems.

Acknowledgements

The origins of this book go back several years to Lars Reuterswärd's idea, as the then Director of Mistra Urban Futures (MUF), to establish Fair, Green and Dense as cornerstones of MUF's work. Accordingly, 'position papers' were commissioned to review the respective literatures and to examine their potential relevance for MUF, as the basis for engagement with the Centre's research platforms and then to inform the work programme. That initiative was abandoned but on becoming MUF Director in late 2014, I realised that the material had potential for publication in a different form and with a different remit as explained in Chapter One.

Nevertheless, bringing this book to fruition has proved very challenging. The original Green Cities paper was committed elsewhere, so I have written an entirely fresh chapter. Jaan-Henrik Kain, the original author of an incomplete draft of the Dense Cities paper, was no longer available to do more work. Accordingly, James Waters was commissioned to produce what is now Chapter Two on Accessible Cities, although he has drawn on two subsections of Kain's original draft with the latter's generous permission, which we hereby acknowledge gratefully. Susan Parnell is the only one remaining of the original three authors, and has revised and updated Chapter Four to suit this volume. She originally commenced work with Lars Lilled, then of Gothenburg City, but the actual writing is hers. Lars' contribution in the earlier stages is fully acknowledged.

In addition to the chapter authors, Henrietta Palmer, Deputy Scientific Director at MUF, joined the enterprise and read and commented in detail on all three chapters and co-authored Chapter Five. Jan Riise also read chapters One and Three. Thanks also to Hayley Leck for feedback on Chapter Three. Malcolm Kelsey, of the Geography Department at Royal Holloway, University of London, drew Figure 3.1, while Marty Legros of MUF prepared Table 3.1. Particular thanks are due to Stina Hansson of MUF, who undertook the final copyediting and harmonisation of the manuscript very professionally under considerable time pressure.

Finally, I thank Laura Vickers and her team at Policy Press for their interest in the venture and supporting the preparation and production processes so effectively. The work reported in these pages was funded by Mistra, the Gothenburg Consortium and Sida. In line with the funders' mandate to maximise access to the knowledge produced, Mistra Urban Futures has paid the Open Access fee in order to make the electronic version of this book available free of charge worldwide.

Foreword

This book comes out at a time when cities appear, at last, to be recognised by national and international policy makers and public opinion in many countries for their significant contribution to wealth creation and human well-being. For a long time since the early nineteenth century in Europe, urban concentrations of population and industry were seen with suspicion by politicians and intellectuals who saw in them the embodiment of social ills such as poverty, crime, pollution, and the gradual destruction of a pristine natural environment. From the second half of the twentieth century onwards, this attitude permeated much of the combined international efforts to channel aid to poorer countries. Flows of migrants arriving in cities were seen as presaging social demands or even revolts and growing concentrations of undesirable evils. Very rarely were they seen as making a positive contribution to a national economy that was already changing, partly as a result of trade, specialisation and higher incomes. In a small number of cases, such flows responded to major natural disasters or human-made calamities such as wars. Only a handful of autocratic countries managed to contain the major structural shifts from rural-based basic subsistence around farming or fishing, to more productive occupations and the search (not always successful, it is true) by people of most social classes for better education and health services, and better-paid jobs.

Sandwiched between the rather triumphant announcements of the Paris Agreement on Climate Change in December 2015 and the

Habitat III meeting of nations states in Quito in October 2016 focused on a 'New Urban Agenda' to face urban challenges, this book elegantly captures the major concerns of the international community on the role cities can play in the future of humanity. On one side, there is the issue of the contribution of a growing concentration of people in around three per cent of the planet's area marked by the highest ever levels of consumption of material goods, associated emissions and waste. And, on the other, there is the more upbeat dimension historically highlighted by city advocates as places embodying individual freedom, collective creativity, and high productivity, an idea that today finds fewer opponents partly thanks to the fact that more urban dwellers are likely to have been born in cities than in remote villages.

But the challenges ahead, as this book's authors point out, are significant. Cities are here to stay, despite the occasional despotic attempts to evict people or keep them out at the cost of hundreds or even thousands of lives. For the foreseeable future, cities will continue to house a growing share of us, the jobs that sustain us, and the services we use. Cities have simply proven to be better at this than dispersed patterns of population. But they have also shown to be places of waste, both human and material, where not every human being living is able to make the most of their potential, and where increasingly higher levels of material consumption lead to more waste that has to be absorbed by natural sinks that will soon exhaust their capacity. Unfortunately, they are also increasingly places of inequality, where some are able to accumulate material wealth (and the power associated with it) much faster and in much bigger volume than others. This may be intrinsic to capitalism rather than a quality of cities, but it is aided by poor city leadership allowing growing differences to find physical expressions in gated communities housing the rich and the middle classes, in motorway toll-lanes exclusively for private cars, in bans of non-motorised transport that the poor can afford, and in poor quality housing in crime-ridden neighbourhoods many miles from jobs where the poorest are forced to live.

Written by scholars of the highest international standing, this concise volume argues that, in the face of these considerable challenges, the complexity of urbanisation is best examined through three analytical lenses: the capacity of cities to provide access (to opportunities, to places), their capacity to foster a greener national economy and a greener, more environmentally sustainable planet, and their capacity to ensure that the societies in which they are located are fairer, and provide opportunities to all current and future residents.

The title of the book says it all: the search for sustainability involves twin efforts both in cities and in society. Despite its somewhat unfortunate martial tone, a quote from the 'Zero Draft' of the New Urban Agenda offers an apt metaphor for the challenges that await all of us who are concerned with the wellbeing of all citizens and our planet: "the battle for sustainable development will be won or lost in cities".

Julio D Dávila
Professor of Urban Policy and International Development
Director, Development Planning Unit,
University College London

May 2016

1
INTRODUCTION: SUSTAINABLE CITIES IN SUSTAINABLE SOCIETIES

David Simon

Sustainable urbanisation has moved to the forefront of debate, research and policy agendas over recent years. There are numerous reasons for this, differing in precise combination across countries and regions. Among the most important of these is a growing appreciation of the implications of rapid urbanisation now occurring in China, India and many other low- and middle-income countries with historically low urbanisation levels. Much of this urbanisation is emulating unsustainable resource-intensive patterns from high-income countries, with the demonstration effect enhanced by greater global mobility, globalisation of architectural and urban planning consultancies and construction firms, and the power of the media and information and communications technologies.

Similarly, the related challenges posed to urban areas and regions worldwide by climate/environmental change have now become more widely understood and the urgency of taking action increasingly appreciated, even in poor cities and towns. This constitutes remarkable progress from a situation of just a few years ago when such arguments fell on deaf ears since the problems were held to be too distant in the future compared to meeting immediate demands for scarce resources. Almost everywhere, the realities of fluctuating and unpredictable weather patterns, and especially the increasing frequency and severity of extreme events, as well as extensive loss of life and both economic and environmental damage, are changing perceptions among elected urban representatives, officials and residents alike.

A key marker of the increasing importance of urban issues is how they have risen up the international agenda. This is symbolised by the inclusion of a specifically urban Goal (no 11) – to make cities inclusive, safe, resilient and sustainable – in the set of 17 Sustainable Development Goals (SDGs) adopted by the UN at the 2015 General Assembly. The SDGs have now replaced the Millennium Development Goals (MDGs) from 2016 (Parnell, Chapter Four, this volume; Simon, Chapter Three, this volume). Unlike the MDGs, the SDGs were formulated through an unprecedentedly lengthy and diverse consultative process involving national and sub-national governments, international agencies, non-governmental organisations (NGOs), the private sector and community organisations in every country. Importantly, too, the Goals apply to all countries, regardless of per capita income or position on the Human Development Index. This demonstrates the shared fate of humankind in the face of sustainability challenges, be these related to inadequate access to the resources for meeting basic needs and an acceptable quality of life or to excessive consumption and the associated health, resource depletion and environmental problems.

Symbolically, too, given their consistently growing demographic, economic, environmental and socio-cultural importance worldwide, cities and other sub-national entities were mentioned explicitly for the first time in the Paris Agreement reached at COP21 of the United Nations Framework Convention on Climate Change (UNFCCC) in Paris in early December 2015. This gives special recognition to the role of urban areas in meeting the climate change challenges. Meanwhile the New Urban Agenda, launched officially at the Habitat III global summit in Quito, Ecuador, in October 2016, and which will shape global efforts to promote more sustainable urbanisation and urban areas for the following 20 years, has been under active preparation through UN member states and diverse stakeholder groups worldwide.

That the importance of urban sustainability is now receiving wide recognition represents the first prerequisite for progress towards that objective. However, therein lies a double paradox. While it might at first sight seem feasible to make well-resourced, orderly towns and cities in high-income countries more sustainable, changing the entrenched resource-intensive, high-consumption economic processes and lifestyles there, and the power relations and vested interests bound up with them, will require immense effort, finance and political will. Conversely, to many people, the widespread poverty, resource and service deficits and chronic traffic congestion of large, fast-growing cities in poor countries represent the ultimate challenge or 'wicked urban problem'. Yet, although powerful vested interests exist there too and can be highly resistant to change, the example of Lagos under the previous governor, Babatunde Fashola, demonstrates how an energetic champion untainted by personal corruption, committed to the cause and possessing the right connections can bring about remarkable results in a relatively short period, even in the face of some of the most severe problems in any megacity.

Naturally, though, however sustainable or otherwise, cities do not exist as isolated islands of bricks, concrete, steel, glass, tarmac, corrugated iron, wood and cardboard. Indeed, they form integral parts of wider natural and politico-administrative regions, as well as national and supranational entities, on which they depend for resources, waste disposal, human interaction and the circulation of people, commodities and finance. Urban areas can lead or lag in sustainability transitions but ultimately sustainable towns and cities exist only as components of more or less sustainable societies. This is both a truism and shown historically, with evidence accumulating from various ancient urban-based societies on different continents (Simon and Adam-Bradford, 2016). This further complexity creates 'boundary problems' since the interactive systems span often numerous administrative areas, complicating yet further what are already complex development, economic, environmental, political, social and technical challenges.

Sustainability is itself a complex and contested notion at all spatial scales, containing diverse elements, some relatively easy to measure and others more qualitative. Moreover, like development, sustainability has the triple characteristics of being simultaneously a normative aspiration, a state of being and the means of attaining that state. It has been theorised, appropriated, used and abused in numerous discourses and practical applications, to the point that some critics claim that – also like development – it has lost any usefulness. Some of these complexities are examined in the urban context in Chapter Three, especially the differences between 'weak' and 'strong' sustainability discourses, policies and practices and the need to integrate economic, socio-cultural and environmental dimensions within holistic approaches.

Distinctiveness of this book

While the literature on various aspects of urban sustainability is substantial and growing apace, the immediate justification for this book is its originality and the absence of any comparable volume. Most existing books adopt specific conceptual approaches, deal with particular countries or regions, and/or focus heavily on environmental and/or economic aspects. Many of the books on equity/fairness within sustainability (such as Agyeman, 2013; Agyeman et al, 2003; Atkinson and Wade, 2014) are not specifically urban in focus. Some of these issues, as well as broader concerns relating to urban inequality and poverty, are well covered elsewhere, with a range of theoretical and more applied emphases (see, for instance, Myers, 2011, 2016; Pieterse, 2008; Pieterse and Simone, 2013; Satterthwaite and Mitlin, 2014; Tannerfeldt and Ljung, 2006). However, the early books on sustainability challenges in cities, which appeared some two decades ago (such as Pugh, 1996; 2000) reflect the thinking and concerns of that time, whereas debates and our understanding have moved on. Many more recent urban titles provide general introductions to the role of urban planners or urban planning principles and practice, nowadays increasingly emphasising sustainability (for example, Rydin, 2011).

Others focus on particular aspects of planning (city centres, neighbourhoods) or the UK (for instance, Flint and Raco, 2011; Imrie and Lees, 2014). Hodson and Marvin (2014) has some similarities to this book, especially with respect to elements of green agendas, but also a focus on energy and other themes. Accordingly, the importance of and reasons for organising this book around the three key dimensions of sustainable cities, namely accessibility, greenness and fairness, are set out below. The final section of this chapter provides an overview of the rest of the book.

This compact book seeks to make a signal contribution to the understanding of sustainable urbanisation agendas through authoritative interventions contextualising, assessing and explaining clearly the relevance and importance of three central dimensions of sustainable towns and cities everywhere, namely that they should be accessible, green and fair. These three dimensions inform the work of Mistra Urban Futures (MUF), an international research centre on sustainable urbanisation based in Gothenburg, Sweden, and operating through transdisciplinary co-design/co-production research platforms there, in Skåne (southern Sweden), in Greater Manchester (UK), Cape Town (South Africa) and Kisumu (Kenya). These platforms bring together groups of researchers from universities and research institutes, parastatals, local and regional authorities and official agencies to identify shared problems and to undertake joint research to find and then implement solutions. A new partnership in Asia and/or Latin America is planned in 2016/7 in order to establish a research presence in most continental regions, which will enhance MUF's ability to undertake comparative research into principles and guidelines of good practice and thereby to influence urban sustainability agendas at all spatial scales.

In order to assess the state of the art and to inform the second phase of its research programme in terms of intellectual coherence, MUF has undertaken substantive reviews of the existing literature in relation to accessible, green and fair cities. The nature of this work lends itself to wider distribution in order to inform evolving urban sustainability debates and policy dialogues worldwide. Many of these debates came together in the preparatory process for the

5

Habitat III summit in October 2016 and the 'New Urban Agenda' for the following two decades within the UN System and – at least as important – outside it. That constitutes the context and rationale for this book as local, national and international policymakers and practitioners grapple with the twin challenges of building numerous new urban areas (sometimes dubbed 'the cities yet to come') and new urban segments in growing cities while also redesigning old urban areas and segments in accordance with emerging principles of good urban sustainability practice in different contexts around the world. Equally, these principles are increasingly finding a central place in university courses and professional training modules on sustainable cities and urban design. Hence this book should also be of value in the classroom.

The three thematic chapters survey the origins, evolution and diverse interpretations and applications of the respective dimensions – accessible, green and fair – in different contexts internationally and how they inform current debates and discourses, as set out below. In order to provide more integrated coverage and minimise overlap, cross-referencing has been included where appropriate.

In order to enhance the accessibility and usefulness of this book, a selective annotated list of relevant websites provides information on internet resources in different aspects of the theory, policy and practice of urban sustainability to the diverse audiences at which this book is aimed, not least urban practitioners.

Organisation of the contents

In Chapter Two, 'Accessible cities: from urban density to multidimensional accessibility', James Waters advocates the concept of 'accessible cities', where accessibility is the freedom or ability to obtain goods and services and urban opportunities of various kinds to facilitate human wellbeing. Multiple dimensions of the concept are discussed, as well as how it might be achieved in different contexts. In these terms, accessibility constitutes an advance over density, a more limited but widely used term – not least within World Bank and UN-HABITAT discourses and policy documents over many years – to describe a key urban characteristic in diverse conceptual and normative framings that include density of social networks and employment and other opportunities. In physical terms, purported benefits of high-density development include efficiency and reduced environmental impact, agglomeration and economic benefits, as well as improved social equity but the evidence is mixed and trade-offs occur. Moreover, in some contexts, especially within poor areas of certain South and Southeast Asian metropolises, excessive population density is problematic. Accordingly, this chapter reflects the intellectual journey of MUF over recent years, having initially adopted the UN-HABITAT focus on density but now advocating multifaceted accessibility – which also chimes with the appropriate mobility/accessibility target and indicator in SDG 11.

In Chapter Three, 'Green cities: from tokenism to incrementalism and transformation', David Simon picks up the discussion commenced in the opening section above in explaining how sustainability concerns in relation to urban areas have arisen, evolved and been applied over time and in different socio-spatial contexts. Utopian thinking and urban design, as manifest, for instance in the Garden Cities Movement, date back to the late nineteenth and early twentieth centuries. Explicit urban greening initiatives can be traced back to the 1980s, although its widespread emergence in discourse and practice is much more recent. The diversity of meanings and associations attached to urban greening – indicative of its appeal in numerous contexts – is examined. Various 'weak' or instrumental approaches to urban greening can be distinguished from 'strong' versions that imply more fundamental transitions and transformations. In this regard, deployment of a threefold division of socio-economic, socio-technical and socio-/social-ecological analytical frames is helpful in aiding understanding. The value of the ecosystem services approach to valuing natural assets within urban areas is assessed, including in relation to green and green–blue infrastructural agendas.

A key driver behind the recent popularisation of city greening initiatives is the imperative of addressing climate change and reducing disaster risk (DRR).

Conventional thinking has bifurcated climate change actions into tackling mitigation versus promoting adaptation (see, for instance, Bicknell et al, 2009; Bulkeley, 2013; Bulkeley et al, 2013). Recent evidence shows that this is an artificial division and that carefully targeted interventions can achieve both and also provide health and other co-benefits. Paradoxically, too, a portfolio of individually modest and incremental interventions can have aggregate effects where the whole becomes more than the sum of the parts and hence has important transformative value. Nevertheless, the challenges of political will and resources to move beyond key thresholds of investment and inertia are very real in urban areas of all kinds and degrees of socio-technical sophistication. Conversely, grand high-tech eco-city schemes may prove elitist and of very limited replicability and longer-term sustainability, at least to the majority of poor urban residents.

Susan Parnell starts Chapter Four, entitled 'Fair cities: imperatives in meeting global sustainable developmental aspirations', with questions about what an increasingly urban world implies for fairness at the national or global scale in the twenty-first century. She then traces divergent and contradictory intellectual and practice-based traditions that the notion of fairness in the city implies, including work on urban equity (rights, opportunity, access, affordability); justice (electoral, procedural, distributional, and enforcement); redistribution (urban welfare and post conflict); the public good, the good city and the right to the city. The central argument is that ideas and practices about fairness and social, economic, environmental and spatial justice in the city vary over time and space. On the one hand, there is appropriate concern about rising exclusion and the withdrawal of social protection in some centres (typically in older, more affluent cities) and from new urban nodes (largely in the global South). On the other hand, counter-tendencies and new innovations support the utopian aspiration that cities will provide a better future for the millions of new residents who will call them home.

The book ends with a substantive concluding chapter, in which Henrietta Palmer and David Simon pull together and assess the central strands of the book's intellectual and practice-oriented arguments about accessible, green and fair cities. They relate these to the recurrent utopian thinking within urban planning and design, highlighting the challenges that these imply in relation to operationalising a coherent, if not truly holistic, urban sustainability agenda in different contexts.

References

Agyeman, J., Bullard, R.D. and Evans, B. (eds) (2003) *Just sustainabilities: Development in an unequal world*, Harvard, MA: MIT Press.

Agyeman, J. (2013) *Introducing just sustainabilities*, London: Zed Books .

Atkinson, H. and Wade, R. (2014) *The challenge of sustainability: Linking politics, education and learning*, Bristol: Policy Press.

Bicknell, J., Dodman, D. and Satterthwaite, D. (eds) (2009) *Adapting cities to climate change: Addressing and understanding the development challenges*, London: Earthscan.

Bulkeley, H. (2013) *Cities and climate change*, London and New York: Routledge.

Bulkeley, H., Castán Broto, V., Hodson, M. and Marvin, S. (eds) (2013) *Cities and low carbon transitions*, London and New York: Routledge.

Flint, J. and Raco, M. (eds) (2011) *The future of sustainable cities: Critical reflections*, Bristol: Policy Press.

Hodson, M. and Marvin, S. (eds) (2014) *After sustainable cities?*, London and New York: Routledge.

Imrie, R. and Lees, L. (2014) *Sustainable London? The future of a global city*, Bristol: Policy Press.

Myers, G. (2011) *African cities: Alternative visions of urban theory and practice*, London: Zed Books.

Myers, G. (2016) *Urban environments in Africa: A critical analysis of environmental politics*, Bristol: Policy Press.

Pieterse, E. (2008) *City futures: Confronting the crisis of urban development*, London: Zed Books.

Pieterse, E. and Simone, A.M. (eds) (2013) *Rogue urbanism: Emergent African cities*, Johannesburg: Jacana.

Pugh, C. (1996) *Sustainability, the environment and urbanization*, London and Sterling, VA: Earthscan.

Pugh, C. (2000) *Sustainable cities in developing countries*, London and Sterling, VA: Earthscan.

Rydin, Y. (2011) *The purpose of planning: Creating sustainable towns and cities*, Bristol: Policy Press.

Satterthwaite, D. and Mitlin, D. (2014) *Reducing urban poverty in the global South*, London and New York: Routledge.

Simon, D. and Adam-Bradford, A. (2016) 'Archaeology and contemporary dynamics for more sustainable and resilient cities in the peri-urban interface', in B. Maheshwari, V.P. Singh and B. Thoradeniya (eds) *Balanced urban development: Options and strategies for liveable cities*, Water Science and Technology Library 72, Dordrecht and Heidelberg: Springer, pp 57–83.

Tannerfeldt, G. and Ljung, P. (2006) *More urban, less poor*, London and Sterling, VA: Earthscan.

2

ACCESSIBLE CITIES: FROM URBAN DENSITY TO MULTIDIMENSIONAL ACCESSIBILITY

James Waters

Introduction

This chapter explores what makes a city accessible, both within an urban area such that residents are able to access what they require to attain wellbeing, as well as from outside in order that wider goals such as efficiency, wellbeing, innovation and enterprise or wider sustainability are achieved. This explicitly frames urban areas as integrated with the larger hinterlands of city regions and beyond, as discussed in Chapter One. The first section of this chapter highlights how density influences these different goals in numerous ways, although the exact relationships are often complex and contested. Finding flaws in a singular focus on density, the chapter then considers the need and usefulness of accessibility in urban planning and policy, and how its various dimensions can be measured. Finally the relationships between accessibility and urban form are also considered, and future research directions suggested.

The second section provides a brief history of, and surveys current debates around, urban density, what it means and how it can be measured; the third section discusses what makes an 'accessible city', how that can be measured, and the various dimensions of accessibility; and the fourth section points to future research directions, incorporating state of the art reflections from cities across the world.

Urban density

Concerns with the health and social problems associated with 'excessive' urban density in particular contexts date from the Industrial Revolution in eighteenth to nineteenth century Europe, and provided an important stimulus to the rise of urban planning as a discipline in the late nineteenth century. Unsurprisingly, therefore, the issue of how to address urban density has long been a focus of planners and urban scholars, not least through the visionary master plans of Ebenezer Howard, Le Corbusier and Frank Lloyd Wright (Parnell, Chapter Four, and Simon, Chapter Three, this volume). This is partly because urban areas have the potential to reduce individuals' environmental impact and contribute to regional sustainability, facilitate social cohesion and equity, create opportunities for innovation and economic improvement and generate rich cultural heritage. Densification has been promoted to achieve each of these goals, but also has the potential to affect each of these agendas negatively. This section starts with a discussion of state of the art definitions and measurements, investigates the evidence for the relationship between density and these issues, and finally examines how we might 'make density work'.

Definitions and measures of urban density

Given the diverse meanings of density, it is important to define the concept. Furthermore, density may not just be an end in itself, but may be a means towards broader ends such as connectivity, social vitality and convenience (Turok, 2011).

Different terms, such as crowding, compactness, sprawl, or intensity are used in association with density (see Boyko and Cooper, 2011). Essentially, density is a combination of physical structures (housing) and the actual resident population (Whitehead, 2008). However, the term is surrounded by vagueness, given the different types of density considered (for example, urban, dwelling, people), how that density is defined, and how data are collected, summarised and analysed. Furthermore, much research suggests that people have a strong preference for lower density, while policy in many cities and countries and by agencies such as the World Bank advocates higher densities in the name of more sustainable living (Boyko and Cooper, 2011). Nevertheless, many architects, urban designers, developers, local authority planners and policymakers use the concept and so it is important to understand its meanings and usage.

The simplest measure of density is population density, or the number of people living per unit area. Alternatively physical structures may be considered by measuring the number of dwellings per hectare as in residential density (Plates 2.1, 2.2 and 2.3). This, however, neglects the size and number of habitable rooms in those dwellings, and so the floor area ratio can be used, which is the total floor area of dwellings divided by the land area on which they are built. Alternatively, employment density focuses on the economy. Figures may be gross (including areas of land not related to the figure such as roads or infrastructure), net (excluding such areas), or weighted (assigning weight equal to the share of the population for each area to derive an average). Critically, different professions will use different measures and are aware of the potential for confusion (Boyko and Cooper, 2011; Dempsey et al, 2012).

Plate 2.1: Manhattan borough in New York City (USA), parts of Tokyo (Japan), Singapore and Hong Kong (pictured) have some of the highest residential densities in formal housing in the world by virtue of numerous high rise apartment blocks. These cater for a range of income categories, right up to the elite, with social amenities also in close proximity. (Photo © David Simon)

Plate 2.2: The highest residential densities in informal housing are found in many shantytowns and so-called slums in large cities in the global South. Rio de Janeiro, Brazil, (pictured) is distinctive in terms of the close juxtaposition of high density favelas and middle income apartments (Photo © David Simon)

Plate 2.3: The lowest residential densities are found in high income suburbs worldwide, characterised by large double-storey mansions or single story bungalow/villa houses on extensive plots. Middle-class housing, as here in Ensenada, Mexico, generally occupies smaller plots but densities are still comparatively low (Photo © David Simon)

Although dwelling density and population density are the most widely used indicators, the authors identify five kinds of density and have generated the following taxonomy:

- built form (for example, dwelling or infrastructure density)
- natural form (for example, density of green space)
- static form (for example, road density)
- mobile material form (for example, traffic density)
- people – individual and social/organisational (for example, population density, employment density).

Other criticisms include that density is as much perceived as it is purely a spatial concept: in contexts of overcrowding, perceived density becomes important for issues of urban design and human wellbeing. Therefore, there is a need to consider 'soft' as well as 'hard' measures of urban density, including perception, behaviour and needs. Finally, in order to capture the influence of 'density' on individuals' behaviour and urban dynamics, we need to consider the quality and context of immediate and surrounding environments, as well as preferences and cultural norms as to what is acceptable for urban living (Churchman, 1999; Boyko and Cooper, 2011).

Recent studies have demonstrated the potential of multi-measure and more complex indices. In an investigation into pedestrian flows and dwelling density, Pafka (2013) showed that this density measure is not enough to capture streetlife intensity and that multivariate models are therefore needed. Another issue is the 'vertical space problem', and capturing the distribution of people in vertical residential structures. Accordingly, Perdue (2013) develops a 'personal space measure', while Dovey and Pafka (2014) seek to clarify the links between key concepts and bring together three measures – buildings, populations and open space. Using a loose framework of assemblage theory, their model provides a basis to rethink density as a 'multiplicitous assemblage'. Finally Lee and colleagues (2015) develop a compact city index that is internationally applicable. These state-of-the-art developments indicate the complexity of urban density but also how far the science has come.

Furthermore, the functional density of a city may be increased through connectivity, diversity and intensity. Connectivity will be discussed later on as it pertains to the accessibility of city functions and services. Diversity relates to the degree of mixed use of space, functions and types of inhabitants. It can be measured through the balance of high/low density housing, small/large buildings, and affordable/high end housing, and also affects accessibility as discussed later. Finally intensity is sometimes used synonymously with density, but specifically relates to the use of space, both built form and activity (Westerink et al, 2013).

Current trends and drivers of densification/de-densification

During the past century, total global urban land area has grown rapidly, doubling in OECD countries since the mid-1950s and increasing five-fold outside the OECD (OECD, 2010). Moreover, the global urban population is set to double in the next 40 years while urban land area is predicted to double in only 20 years (Rode et al, 2014). Despite urbanisation continuing apace worldwide, therefore, and notwithstanding uncertainties surrounding long-term projections, analyses suggest that most urban areas worldwide are declining in *average* density.

Obviously there are regional differences, with urban densities in poorer countries double those in Europe and Japan, which are then double those of the United States, Canada and Australia (Angel et al, 2011). As for changing density, the populations of a representative sample of cities in the global North grew by approximately 5 per cent between 1990 and 2000 while their built-up area grew 30 per cent; the equivalents for the global South were 20 per cent population growth to 40 per cent increase in urbanised land (Angel et al, 2005). The decline in density is therefore greater in the global North, with all 32 sample cities declining. Urban densities, however, decreased in 75 of the 88 Southern cities too (Angel et al, 2011).

Comparing the sprawl patterns of India and China reveals some of the effect of different drivers of de-densification. In China, urban population densities decreased on average by 25 per cent between 1999 and 2005, with built-up land in provincial cities doubling in area (World Bank and the Development Research Center of the State Council, PR China, 2014). Conversely, urban development in India has been characterised by far lower rates of horizontal expansion. This has been attributed to stronger private property rights, weaker local governments and insufficient capacity to develop urban infrastructure, a lack of public incentives and lower foreign investment, keeping development more focused on existing urban areas (Sellers et al, 2009).

More generally, factors influencing densification include land and property markets, construction economics, social factors ('not in my backyard'), lifestyle factors and political forces ('not in my ward'). Planned urban sprawl occurs where formal processes of land acquisition are accompanied or preceded by state-led infrastructure development (for example, China, Korea and Thailand); demand- and speculation-led sprawl are driven by private development along transport corridors connecting cities and broader urban infrastructure is often lacking (for example, India, Indonesia and Vietnam); while alternative urban development pathways and re-densification can occur due to the socio-economic incentives of agglomeration, and the reduced attraction of suburban living as family structures, demographics and modern lifestyles change, as in many European cities (Rode et al, 2014). In each context, there will be a different balance of the role of policies and transactions facilitated through market processes.

Conceptual and theoretical framings of density of and within cities

This section considers some of the main framings of urban density and assesses the evidence for the benefits (and disbenefits) of density. Among mainstream urban policy, compactness is generally hailed as a positive goal for urban planning. The World Bank has argued that 'density makes the difference' (World Bank, 2009) and adopted this as a central tenet of its urban policy over many years, while densification has been promoted to achieve sustainable development within European policy (EEA, 2006). More recent discussions have, however, also highlighted the importance of accessibility (Fang, 2015). Similarly UN-HABITAT (2012) advises city leaders that compact spatial structures will deliver maximum benefit to the public at large with minimum negative impacts. Nevertheless, arguments around the relative benefits of urban density are much less clear.

Most arguments for densification are made around the economic value generated through agglomeration, the economic potential of cities, greater resource efficiency and use of transport and better access to services (Holman et al, 2015). However density also relates to a number of wider issues, including housing affordability, privacy, mental and physical wellbeing, crime, biodiversity and energy use (Boyko and Cooper, 2011). Turok (2011) identifies three key benefits of density: more efficient and intensive use of urban land and infrastructure and reduction of impact of car travel, more productive economies and more vibrant and inclusive communities.

Urban efficiency and environmental impact

The density provided by cities arguably offers means to achieve the wellbeing of citizens while minimising environmental impact. Wider environmental issues are considered in Chapter Three (Simon, this volume), while here the focus is on the interaction between density and efficiency/environmental impact. One of the purported advantages is around mobility, with lower fossil fuel emissions from shorter journeys and lower carbon footprints of development. Proximity also allows public transport to become more viable, as well as cycling or walking, generating health benefits as well as reducing private vehicle use and thereby pollution. Furthermore, the notion of 'transit-oriented development' (TOD) drives development that is physically oriented around public transport stations and reduces travel time/distance further. By mixing pedestrian–oriented development with public transport nodes, the likelihood of people using public transport for out-of-neighbourhood trips and walking/cycling within their neighbourhood increases further (Cervero, 2005). TOD also allows high-density urban areas to reduce energy consumption and air pollution further (UN-HABITAT, 2013).

More generally, car ownership is a key factor in determining levels of emissions, with evidence from the UK that increased density reduces levels of car ownership. Dempsey et al (2012) found a clear association between respondents residing in or near UK city centres and lower car ownership. Across larger cities worldwide, many studies have now shown the link between urban form and both transport energy use and carbon emissions. There is up to a ten-fold difference in transport-related carbon emissions between the most energy intensive sprawling cities and energy efficient compact cities (Newman and Kenworthy, 1999 in UN-HABITAT, 2013; Rode et al, 2014).

Energy advantages can come through innovation and green design, as a product of high-density living. In 'smart cities' discourses and designs, digital technologies or information and communication technologies (ICT) are used to enhance urban services, reduce costs and resource consumption, and engage more effectively with citizens (Simon, Chapter Three, this volume). Land use can be intensified in high density areas, with a greater mix of uses, and infrastructure becoming more efficient. With roads, water, sewers and storm water drainage not needing to be extended as far, it can take development pressure off agricultural and industrial land as well as existing green space and improve urban quality of life as a result (Boyko and Cooper, 2011). Furthermore, local open spaces have been found to be valued more highly in high-density areas than outside cities (LSE, 2006).

On the other hand, greater density does not always reduce the need for private car travel (Holman et al, 2015) and can actually cause traffic congestion and parking problems, as well as a larger number of road accidents. Construction of high-density buildings can also cause pedestrian congestion, particularly around public transportation. Within the home, there is evidence from China that compact forms, especially with little access to green space or water bodies, may increase household energy consumption (Ye et al, 2015) but analysis in the UK found a weaker statistical association (Dempsey et al, 2012). More energy will also be used in the construction of high-density buildings, particularly skyscrapers. With regard to land use, disadvantages include a lack of public open space and a reduced ability of the urban area to cope with rainfall and air pollution. The survey of UK households mentioned above found that parks and green spaces tend to be smaller in high-density areas, are of a lower quality and are used less. These levels of use of green space are generally mediated by factors of perceived safety and of lack of maintenance (Dempsey et al, 2012).

In regions such as sub-Saharan Africa, there is rapid and widespread conversion of natural areas into urbanised land, often through low-density sprawl as much as high-density intensified development (Schäffler and Swilling, 2013). Hence the relationship with density is unclear. On the other hand, there is good evidence from European urban development. For example, higher urban densities in the UK were strongly associated with reduced green space coverage as well as hampered ecological functions such as regulation of water and temperature regimes and carbon sequestration (Dempsey et al, 2012). In the future it will become more difficult to place and build new high-density buildings that retain green spaces among already dense urban areas. The relative efficiency benefits of urban density therefore appear to be tempered by urban design and can result in congestion, increased household energy use and a lack of green space. Unfortunately solid evidence on this trend could not be found from the global South but high density development will almost certainly threaten green space unless appropriately designed for and enforced.

Agglomeration and economic benefits

Evidence suggests that high-density development is significantly cheaper compared with funding the infrastructure, maintenance and operating costs of sprawling cities (Rode et al, 2014). For example, the World Bank calculates that compact city development in China could save up to US $1.4 trillion in infrastructure spending, equivalent to 15 per cent of the country's 2013 GDP (World Bank and the Development Research Center of the State Council, PR China, 2014).

These savings would allow greater investment in better quality amenities and building materials, thereby encouraging people to spend more time and money in the area, thus generating a critical mass of people to support services and attract further leisure and retail uses. For example, the City of Cape Town's Densification Policy (2012) proposes that a renewal of older urban fabric could not only allow modern energy, water and waste treatment to be installed and improve public transport but a larger resident population would also increase demand for retail and consumer services and make cultural and arts venues more viable. In this way, they propose that densification would lead to efficiency benefits and generate a cultural pull to the area.

High densities are also promoted because of the economic return on investment and the economies of scale in services and markets that are possible. The high concentration of people promotes a city's economic efficiency, productivity and employment opportunities. Furthermore, the concentration of people and businesses in an area has been shown to foster innovation as it facilitates flows of information that increase the value of services (Boyko and Cooper, 2011; Turok, 2011).

There is, however, also evidence of negative economic consequences of high density. High-density buildings and infrastructure often cost more to build and maintain in higher-density areas (see Boyko and Cooper, 2011). Due to highly valued land, residents can be deprived of recreation space and the relative prices for dwellings, goods and services may be higher (LSE, 2006), although the complex impacts on cost of living and affordability of housing are explored with regard to social equity issues below. Comprehensive empirical evidence suggests that arguments around agglomeration economies are too simple and we need to take into account their dynamic nature as well as spatial heterogeneity within each urban area (Dempsey et al, 2012). Furthermore, most of the evidence on economic advantages and disadvantages of urban density comes from countries such as the US, Australia or the UK (Alexander, 1993; Troy, 1996; and LSE, 2006 in Boyko and Cooper, 2011), is likely to differ in each context and so requires contextual understanding of benefits and disbenefits.

Social equity and wellbeing

The social impacts of high-density urban areas are diverse and the relative benefits for social equity are contested. Aspects of this framing are covered in greater detail by Parnell (Chapter Four, this volume), but the specific linkage with urban density is explored here. Given greater mixing of society and housing type, there is evidence for increased affordability in dense areas. Meanwhile the greater number of people living in an area may make it safer, more diverse, accessible and liveable (Boyko and Cooper, 2011). Positive social interaction may be supported by high-density living (Dempsey et al, 2011), leading to increased social support and community attachment as well as disadvantages such as dependency on the elevator (Churchman and Ginsberg, 1984; Churchman, 1999; Boyko and Cooper, 2011). Similarly, having a supply of resources and housing, a greater choice of peers, especially for children, and proximity of services for those lacking private transport have been found to boost liveability and attachment in Israel and other national contexts (van Vliet, 1985; Churchman, 1999).

Conversely, high-density housing can have social and psychological disadvantages. While potentially bringing a sense of community and social support, the lack of space can also cause living environments to be cramped, noisy and lacking in privacy (Churchman, 1999). This can impinge on the appearance and aesthetics of the physical environment, thereby reducing senses of place. The overshadowing from close proximity of buildings may mean that parents are less able to supervise children, while delinquent behaviour is less noticed, causing an increase in crime. Psychologically, studies have also shown stress, anxiety and social withdrawal, possibly as a result of decreased sense of community (Boyko and Cooper, 2011; 2013). It is important to note that it is hard to equate these effects with absolute density figures, as what is 'liveable' in one social and cultural context will not be in another. What appears to be important is not just actual density but the type of development. In Helsinki, residents can find sensitive infill developments rather attractive and aesthetically positive (Schmidt-

Thomé et al, 2013). Generalisations of urban density on social impacts therefore need to be locally contextualised.

From a social equity perspective, the evidence is equally mixed. The benefits of dense urban living derive from having a range of key services, open space and employment opportunities within walking distance (Power and Burdett, 1999). Density may make key services accessible, especially for groups such as the unemployed, older people or young families (Dempsey et al, 2012), and allow weaker groups in the labour market to improve their access to employment. However, high urban densities sometimes reinforce social inequity and segregation and can mean that the relative prices of goods, services and dwellings are higher (Boyko and Cooper, 2011; 2013). Santiago de Chile demonstrates that it is possible for metropolitan-scale infill development and increasing density levels to help contain urban sprawl and produce more sustainable mobility patterns, albeit at the cost of increasing disparities between areas of the city (Aquino and Gainza, 2014).

Trade-offs and political context

The combination of advantages and disadvantages linked to features of urban density was manifested in the pursuit of an 'optimal city size' in the 1970s. This research revealed that there were efficiency and marginal return benefits from increasing agglomeration, localisation and scale economies, but larger cities were also characterised by diseconomies of scale as well as challenges of congestion and pollution, among others. No clear-cut tipping point could be established within or between countries and as early as 1972, Richardson concluded that such discussions of optimal city size were theoretically unsound and the evidence was ambiguous (Richardson, 1972; Parnell and Simon, 2014).

Furthermore, advantages in one sphere may trade off against benefits in another, while political agendas behind pro-densification arguments may lead to selectivity in the evidence presented (Holman et al, 2015).

There are two main areas of trade-off: between economic efficiency gains and environmental sustainability and trade-offs within the social dimension. With respect to the former, trade-offs that can occur include those between efficiency of infrastructure provision and reduced car use and reduced affordability and green space, as in British Columbia (Alexander and Tomalty, 2002); between urban production and enterprise investment; negative impacts on affordability, green space and crime rates, as in Taiwan (Lin and Yang, 2006); and between compactness and affordability, as in Germany (Thinh et al, 2002). Socially, the two main dimensions of social sustainability – social equity and sustaining communities – often work in opposite directions with increasing density. While some social aspects improve with density (for example, access to services and non-motorised transport), others worsen (for example, provision of green space, feelings of insecurity and social interaction) (Bramley and Power, 2009; Dempsey et al, 2012). Likewise, aspects of social equity such as social segregation may improve while others such as availability of affordable housing decrease (Burton, 2000).

When densification debates focus on urban efficiency and innovation, therefore, there is a risk that they go only as far as intensifying ecological modernisation approaches,[1] narrowing the debate on sustainable cities and possibly at the expense of social issues and wider environmental sustainability.

The political context may also have a significant influence on density/urban efficiency and the issue of whose interests are being served must be considered. Pro-densification arguments are often backed by professionals invoking the urban design-led discourse, as in the UK (for example, Power and Burdett, 1999), based on principles rather than empirical evidence, and often with density taking on an institutional character. The new urbanism debate and urban renaissance in the US have also taken on this notion, informed by a critique of suburbanisation (Holman et al, 2015). By contrast, 'discourses of suspicion' highlight the limitations of market choice in determining built urban form (for example, O'Toole's (2001) criticism of smart growth), and the role of politics may be underplayed in technicist planning-led approaches.

Finally, densification/compact city arguments can actually be used to drive various agendas such as urban competitiveness and profitability even at the expense of local democratic input (Sorensen et al, 2010). In the cases of Toronto and Sydney, this 'political instrumentalisation of the compact city' (Holman et al, 2015) has even been shown to justify differing emphases as the political situation changed, first on residential affordability, and later on reducing expenditures on infrastructure (Searle and Filion, 2011).

City models and applying the principles

Three current paradigms of urban development build on density arguments: compact cities, polycentric cities and smart cities. These address the need to reform sprawling, car-dependent urban development to more compact, public transport-oriented cities. *Compact cities* focus on dense urban forms and patterns. They have been endorsed for many of the positive arguments around urban density above, namely resource efficiency and ability to exploit new technologies, less development on rural land, reduced energy use, lower infrastructure cost, higher quality of life and higher social cohesion. Conversely, the pitfalls of high density mentioned above, including crowding, lack of affordable housing, increase in crime, congestion, loss of green space and pollution, also apply (Echenique et al, 2012; UN-HABITAT, 2012).

The *polycentric city* is designed with a corridor, star or satellite morphology and addresses issues of containing urban growth, creating room for urban biodiversity, making space for vibrant and diverse neighbourhoods and reducing travelling time by concentrating development near easily accessible locations (Westerink et al, 2013). The objective of polycentric cities is to deliver the benefits of both sprawling and compact cities through focusing on centres of social and commercial activity, which work out as communities formed around multiple neighbourhoods. These neighbourhoods include a diversity of private activities and public services within easy proximity so that car use is reduced and public transport and walking/cycling are utilised. In turn, this would increase the sense of place and reduce likelihood of crime.

The third and most recent model is that of so-called *smart cities*, where smart growth allows greater efficiencies through co-ordinating transportation, land speculation, conservation and economic development (Batty et al, 2012). Smart growth is argued to encourage innovation and reorient the private property market, potentially increasing competitiveness through integrating hard infrastructure with knowledge communication and social infrastructure (human and social capital) (Caragliu et al, 2011). However, this model has certain socio-technical underpinnings, being dependent on sophisticated ICTs. Smart city agendas often help to reduce emissions as part of wider sustainability goals (Simon, Chapter Three, this volume).

In order to achieve densification or indeed the specific outcome of any of these three models, three approaches can be distinguished: i) state-driven procedures such as making land available for development (likely at local or regional government); ii) state stimuli to market producers; and iii) fiscal measures to influence household preferences and location choices (Turok, 2011). Making a compact city development plan workable, however, requires the effective management of urban growth, reforming inappropriate building density regulations, engaging with existing urban form to work out how best to sequence, co-ordinate and integrate various developments and introducing regulatory policy instruments to support plans around policies such as car use. It requires an ample supply of housing that will raise considerations regarding design of new housing, combining different forms of housing tenure for social integration and enough attractive external spaces and good public services to make high densities and less living space acceptable.

Even with these steps in place, applying the principles of a compact or smart cities agenda may raise difficulties such as upsetting the existing benefits structure. In order to address the balance of benefits and disbenefits of density in any specific context, plans will need to carefully maintain the quality and extent of living space (Dave, 2010), and mitigate any negative consequences with regard to green space and affordability (Alexander and Tomalty, 2002). Difficult decisions will have to be made regarding composition of housing tenures, types and sizes to suit different groups, which will be aided by participatory planning approaches and learning mechanisms that give greater voice to residents and building managers, as well as local planners and politicians (Turok, 2011; Holman et al, 2015).

Challenging dense cities

Most of the evidence supporting the debates thus far has come from countries in the global North, predominantly the US and the UK. However, given the rapidly changing nature of many cities in the global South, it is critical to consider to what degree these concepts and models are transferable. First, it is important to acknowledge that density will not necessarily, of itself, produce optimal occupation because – especially in many rapidly urbanising contexts – many people live in overcrowded 'slum' or squatment conditions because they are unable to access or afford adequate space, amenities and services (Huchzermeyer, 2011; Simon, 2011). In such contexts, excessive density can constitute part of the problem rather than a solution and the longstanding densification agenda of the World Bank and other agencies fails to take account of such empirical diversity.

Second, these rapidly growing cities often result in large numbers of people in 'slums' and informal settlements, presenting a 'clash of rationalities' for urban planning between techno-managerial and marketised systems and increasingly marginalised populations surviving under informality (Watson, 2009). Ideals of infrastructure development being linked to strategic planning policy that then informs local planning and policy do not necessarily work in many cities in the global South, where infrastructure provision and market-based policies generally guide development (Rode et al, 2014). Furthermore there are different priorities – for instance, basic infrastructure and supply of habitable housing rather than considering privacy or green space quality (Simon, Chapter Three, this volume). However, where there is a lack of planning, institutional creativity and 'bricolage' are found to compensate such that it is not actually an obstacle to the extension of services in unplanned settlements (Criqui, 2015). Given these differences, there is a need for a Southern perspective in planning theory (Watson, 2014).

Higher density, then, is not always an entirely positive goal since, despite its potential as already discussed, the evidence is mixed and there are trade-offs in practice. The concept may be manipulated politically and models such as 'compact cities' will have limited value if not translatable to global South contexts. Accordingly, the case can be made rather to consider 'accessible cities' – cities that may incorporate the positive benefits of urban density, but also focus on access to services, job opportunities, education and housing for the purpose of achieving wellbeing.

Accessible cities

What are 'accessible cities'?

Accessibility is the ability of people to reach goods or services as measured by their availability in terms of physical space, affordability and appropriateness. But accessibility also refers to the provision of services and facilities, job opportunities, education and housing, as well as the means of reaching them. In urban terms, density as examined above is one factor affecting accessibility, but we also need to consider connectivity, diversity and intensity; these links are considered later. Moreover as part of 'accessible cities', broader dimensions, ranging from physical to affordable, to socio-cultural accessibility, need to be considered.

Accessibility refers to the ability of individuals to participate in necessary or desired activities for the wellbeing of humanity. The review of density above revealed the difficulties in finding systematic links between urban density and human wellbeing, including mixed evidence, trade-offs within and between different aspects of density and the politicisation of the topic (Plate 2.4). We therefore turn to accessibility as a facet of cities that relates to increasing human wellbeing.

Plate 2.4: The trade-offs among different forms of accessibility are well illustrated by these informal traders in central Lagos, Nigeria, who locate themselves to maximise passing trade, despite the noise and apparent inconvenience of their stall's site (Photo © David Simon)

This first sub-section describes the history of accessibility as a concept, explores its relation to social sustainability, then introduces key dimensions of accessibility.

History of the concept

From the late 1940s, scholars began to study the ways in which individuals and groups of people access places, other individuals and spatially distributed opportunities in relation to constraints of time, cost and effort (Couclelis, 2000; Couclelis and Getis, 2000, in Tranos et al, 2013). Hansen (1959) and Weibull (1976) were the first to define accessibility systematically (see De Montis and Reggiani 2013). They interpreted accessibility as the potential opportunities which can be reached from a given place by paying a certain generalised space/time-based cost (De Montis and Reggiani, 2013). Hansen focused more on the potential opportunities for interaction, and Morris and colleagues (1979) on activities that could be reached, while Couclelis (2000) addressed the concept more generally as the geographic definition of opportunity (see Tranos et al, 2013). Accessibility, therefore, not only appears to be a useful tool for good practice and planning but also as a means to promote societal wellbeing.

In fact, improving accessibility has recently re-emerged as a central aim of many urban planners (Iacono et al, 2010), focused on transport and physical connectivity, as well as the densification of urban structures through increased mobility and access to urban functions. Many studies have focused on access to public goods, such as public spaces, labour markets or services (see De Montis and Reggiani, 2013). More recent studies have included considerations of connectivity and linking up specific groups of people, for instance the 'creative class' (Knudsen et al, 2007), as well as different civil-society groups and local governments (Satterthwaite, 2010).

Lately, however, with the innovation, spread and merging of telecommunications and digital information technologies, economic, social and cultural activities may be accessed not just via physical transport. These technologies are combining with advances in physical transportation to alter accessibility landscapes (Tranos et al, 2013). Therefore accessibility relates to places, people, opportunities and activities, and through both physical and virtual connections. The following section explores how accessibility relates to social sustainability and, therefore, what dimensions make up an 'accessible city'.

Relation to social sustainability

Beyond mere movement to certain locations in a city, the dimensions of accessible cities are strongly tied to social sustainability. Social sustainability focuses on social issues such as inequality, displacement, liveability and the need for affordable housing (Woodcraft, 2015). Early debates on sustainable cities were associated with limiting ecological footprints through solid waste management or reduced car dependency. Nowadays, however, issues such as access to employment, services and education, as well as cultural values, social cohesion and economic stability are all becoming more relevant (Weingaertner and Moberg, 2014). Chapter Three (Simon, this volume) covers environmental concerns that have been raised in urban development, many of which are also key for environmental sustainability, while Chapter Four (Parnell, this volume) covers some of the social equity issues that pertain to social sustainability. Likewise there is overlap between social sustainability and characteristics of accessible cities, which are explored in more detail below.

Social sustainability has been described as a 'nebulous concept' and there have been numerous reviews and many different categorisations (Bramley et al, 2009; Vallance et al, 2011; Dempsey et al, 2012). Laguna's (2014) comprehensive social sustainability assessment framework includes six key policy areas: housing, transportation, food, leisure and recreation, social cohesion and identity and sense of place. According to Dempsey et al (2011), by contrast, social sustainability objectives include good and equitable access to good-quality services and facilities, social interaction and social networks, feelings of safety, participation in organised activities, feelings of pride/sense of place attachment and community stability.

Social sustainability is also underpinned by two broad concepts: social equity and sustainability of community (Dempsey et al, 2012). Social equity refers to the fair distribution of resources and an avoidance of exclusionary practices, allowing all residents to participate fully in society, socially, economically and politically (Pierson, 2003). Linking to concepts of 'fair' and 'green' cities, cities being 'accessible' means the opposite of areas of social exclusion and inequity where people do not have access to public services and facilities. When access to such services is achieved, territorial justice prevails. Community sustainability refers to the ability of a society/local community to sustain and reproduce itself at an acceptable level of social organisation, with the integration of individual behaviour in a wider collective setting (Bramley et al, 2009).

There is a high degree of overlap between social sustainability and accessible cities since access is a key issue for employment, services and education, affordable housing, transportation, recreation facilities, formal and informal institutions; as well as community relationships and social infrastructure that helps create social equity and community sustainability. Accessibility also relates to the procedural aspects of social sustainability, such as access to stakeholder communication and consultation in development processes, accountable governance and management of policy and planning and social monitoring of the standard-setting process (Bostrom, 2012). The following section describes how accessibility may be measured, before the various dimensions of accessible cities are explored.

Measuring accessibility

Accessibility is in many ways a broader concept than density, which presents challenges for assessment and measurement. It encompasses a variety of dimensions (see next section) and novel methods are often used to measure accessibility, from spatial interaction models to descriptive analysis from survey data, to interlocking network models (Reggiani, 2012; De Montis and Reggiani, 2013).

Within transport and digital accessibility, De Montis and Reggiani (2013) recommend three approaches: digital accessibility; using Complex Networks Analysis (CNA) to measure complex urban systems, with potential accessibility as an indicator; and using Geographic Information Systems (GIS). GIS is becoming an essential tool to measure (transport) accessibility and can generate detailed information on the accessibility of urban opportunities for just one or for many people (Neutens et al, 2010). Other studies have used online surveys to generate an accessibility curve for different transport types (Vasconcelos and Farias, 2012), and GIS can even be combined with methods such as fuzzy logic (Lotfi and Koohsari, 2009). Related measures of the built environment would include location of key services and facilities, public transport routes and provision for walking and cycling (Dempsey et al, 2012).

For many aspects of accessibility, such as physical, affordable housing, ecological/public space, such methods will apply. Broader dimensions however, such as social infrastructure, or power and justice, need to be considered separately.

Dimensions of accessible cities

The notion of 'accessible cities' encompasses much more than transport and mobility, contributing to social sustainability as described above. First, the necessary types of public goods include public spaces, metro systems, labour markets, streets, services and green spaces (De Montis and Reggiani, 2013). In addition, accessible cities must have social infrastructure that allows social equity (which includes affordability) and the formal and informal institutions for individuals to thrive, as well as the power and justice systems to make them accessible. More structurally, accessible cities should have the physical and ecological/ public space for residents to meet their aesthetic, recreational and sense-of-place wants and needs. The following section discusses these dimensions, as well as power and justice as a mediator of access.

Proximity to places and services

Perhaps the most straightforward dimension of accessible cities is the accessibility to places and services through proximity. This aspect also most closely links with density discussions, given that physical proximity is strongly determined by urban form. The most defining features of this include residential and workplace densities, the distribution of functions and degree of mixed use, the level of centralisation and the local-level urban design (Rode et al, 2014). More compact and dense cities increase proximity to locations and services; indeed, local accessibility is an aspect of 'smart mobility' in some frameworks for a smart city (Giffinger et al, 2007).

Residential proximity is most valued by residents for accessibility to social relations and basic daily activities (Haugen, 2012). Another study in Sweden found an 'accessibility paradox', however – that over the study period of ten years, spatial accessibility improved, with average distances both locally and regionally decreasing, whereas travel distance increased (Haugen and Vilhelmson, 2013). In other words, people will go further than necessary for amenity provisions that they desire. This shows the importance of understanding context and agency with regard to the effect of both density (see above) and the determinants of accessibility. This also has challenging implications for policy – that land use planning measures to promote local access may not be sufficient for attaining more sustainable levels of mobility (Haugen and Vilhelmson, 2013).

Accessibility to places and services differs greatly at the intra-urban scale, depending on assets and social networks, and at the inter-urban scale between cities in different parts of a country and internationally. Accessible cities should permit easy access for all urban dwellers to critical services such as education and healthcare, but the question needs to be asked in each context whether it is possible for local government to provide access to all such services, or whether some will be provided through more informal routes. These considerations provided a substantial challenge to the team developing the accessibility indicator for the urban Sustainable Development Goal (SDG 11) during 2013–15, in that it had to be simultaneously meaningful in diverse contexts worldwide and practicable to measure and report on an annual basis to demonstrate progress over the 15-year life of the SDGs (Simon et al, 2016).

Transport

While proximity determines individuals' accessibility to places and services, transport is the mediating factor determining how individuals reach those destinations. With accessibility as the goal, both land use and transport need to be considered in order to facilitate the movement of people, not necessarily cars. Transit-oriented development builds on this principle, characterised by compact patterns adjacent to a public transport node (Plate 2.5). Empirical evidence has shown that comparing node-, density- and accessibility-based views, *access* to important features such as jobs is determined by the interactions between land-use structure and transportation (Cheng et al, 2013). At the urban regional planning level, therefore, accessibility provides a useful framework to integrate transport and land use planning.

Plate 2.5: This minibus terminus in Dakar, Senegal, is a key accessibility hub for this part of the metropolis, linking diverse areas with affordable motor transport (Photo © David Simon)

To a certain extent, physical proximity can be substituted by increasing the speed of travel through urban areas. Good urban transport links can achieve urban compactness in the time aspect through well-networked public transport systems, even if those urban forms are relatively sprawled (Lee et al, 2015). Infrastructural features that achieve what is called 'access by velocity' include the surface coverage of roads, the quality of road and rail networks and other public transport infrastructure. The quality of public service provision and the availability of privately-owned vehicles will obviously also have effects. The mechanisation of transport, associated reduction in mobility costs and widespread introduction of privately-owned cars have allowed cities to de-densify and expand horizontally through suburbanisation in the first place (see Rode et al, 2014).

Private motor transport allows low-density suburban development, but requires much more space for roads. This creates a tension between public transport that requires urban density and private car use that requires space. This is a particular challenge in dense, developing cities where rapid motorisation far outpaces road infrastructure provision or public transport alternatives (Rode et al, 2014). As a result, there is severe traffic congestion in dense Asian cities such as Bangkok, with a lack of road capacity and public transport slow to improve (Barter, 2002), although more recently the Skytrain has helped.

While the introduction of private transport revolutionised individuals' accessibility in the past (and continues to do so in much of the global South), the introduction of infrastructure such as high-speed rail (HSR) is having significant impacts on accessibility today. HSR makes long-distance inter-city relationships possible (Garmendia et al, 2012) but the diverse ways in which HSR is being implemented have different impacts; for instance, the HSR network in China will bring about considerable improvements in accessibility but will also increase inequality of nodal accessibility between eastern, central and western regions, and between cities of different population size (Jiao et al, 2014). Monzón and colleagues (2013) also raise equity concerns that improvements in accessibility produce locational advantages and increase the attractiveness of those cities, thereby enhancing competitiveness and economic growth, but this is limited to urban areas with an HSR station; other surrounding locations receive only limited benefits or may lose out.

Changes in urban accessibility through transport have significant impacts on economic development, inequality, human development and wellbeing and on the environment. Many urban problems such as joblessness, traffic congestion, unaffordable housing and air pollution are linked to accessibility (Cervero, 2005). Particularly in rapidly developing cities in the global South, socio-spatial segregation and inadequate urban transport often represent a barrier for improving livelihood conditions, and can exacerbate income and wealth inequality. Furthermore, because externalities generated through transport such as road accidents, air pollution and displacement disproportionately affect the poor, conventional motorisation in cities can have socially regressive effects. On the other hand, improving accessibility for all through transport will increase the poor's access to goods, services and economic opportunities. More generally, the better and more efficient urban transport overall, the greater the economic benefits through access to goods and services, networking advantages and agglomeration effects mentioned above.

A city's transportation system will affect its environmental impact too. The level of carbon emissions is strongly determined by the mode of transport, with 80 per cent of the increase in global transport emissions since 1970 being due to road vehicles (IPCC, 2014). Linked to the relationship between density and environmental impact raised above, Chapter Three (Simon, this volume) discusses the link between environmental impact and transport in more depth.

Finally these different aspects of urban form, transportation mode and access can be combined in the notion of 'urban accessibility pathways'. Each city will have its own unique urban structure and transportation system but different principal development patterns have evolved that have strong path dependency, and so can be broadly categorised. Rode et al (2014) illustrate the spectrum between car and transit cities, where each accessibility pathway is defined by the degree to which accessibility is based on physical proximity or transport solutions and the degree to which these are private or public transportation. The key is for urban planners to be aware of the socio-economic and environmental impacts of each. Portland, Oregon (US) and the Randstad region of the Netherlands are good examples of where accessibility has become a planning principle. Unless the nuances of transport accessibility are considered, even sustainable mobility policies may miss key impacts such as access for the most vulnerable to economic and social resources (Cucca and Tacchi, 2012) (Plate 2.6).

Plate 2.6: Pedestrianised streets in high density commercial areas like Chinatown in Singapore, maximise accessibility and shopper densities, while increasing pollution-free amenity (Photo © David Simon)

Social infrastructure

Accessible cities will also have the social infrastructure enabling all residents to interact, participate in social groups and organisations and to construct the social networks necessary to build collective resilience and thrive.

Bramley et al's (2009) five-city study in the UK found that interaction with neighbours and participation in groups is more likely at medium urban densities, controlling for other factors, while community participation is not influenced by density. Housing tenure and the social composition of neighbourhoods, however, have a greater influence, and poverty has a greater impact than urban form, for instance, whether residents choose to live there or not. While the provision of community facilities and mixed land use that allows a greater variety of activities are important (Dempsey et al, 2011), accessible cities also require urban planning to take a metropolitan-wide approach, which takes into account the spatial provision of social services and environmental amenities and even the divergent density preferences of both the rich and the poor (Aquino and Gainza, 2014).

Furthermore, urban renewal practices often emphasise economic revival and physical changes, missing the importance of social dynamics. As in Potchefstroom (Tlokwe Municipality) in South Africa, pro-social behaviour patterns between the private sector, community groups and the general public made all the difference in creating an environment that is conducive to sustainability (Meiring, 2013). Social capital and networks are also crucial for resilience, in terms of how those social groups respond in times of crisis or shock (Adger, 2003). Different types of social networks are important for social resilience (Waters, 2013), with membership of community groups a key facet. Accessible cities should therefore consider how urban form and the spatial provision of community facilities allow urban populations to form links between sectors of society and individuals to access social networks and community groups.

Power and justice

Access is also profoundly about power and justice to ensure that accessibility exists for all of the urban population. The politics and economics of urban development mean that there are often lower levels of resource access in deprived areas (Field et al, 2004). At higher scales there will be 'conflicting rationalities' between different role-players in the development of the city that may be hard to resolve (Watson, 2003). These differences may well affect local resource distribution geographically, resulting in differential access for parts of society, and creating the need to ensure locally equitable resource distribution. In the process of gentrification, for example, which often comes with increasing density and aligns with certain political agendas, low-income residents are often pushed out into peripheral, sparsely populated areas with longer commute times (Zhang, 2014) and increased travel costs. Therefore, there is a need to consider how the political and institutional context affects development.

There is also a need to integrate justice into urban planning for accessible cities in order to consider spatial, racial and gender-based inequalities. Research into low-wage labour markets in Chicago, for example, found that households decide on residential location based on jobs, but racial segregation also played an informal role (see Zhang, 2014). While accessible cities certainly require equitable access according to race, gender and population group, one should also be aware of trade-offs between access to services such as transport and environmental pollution. Paradoxically, private transport access in terms of car ownership or low-cost airlines may lead to environmental pollution while policies to contain these environmental impacts may harm social justice, for example through environmental taxation (Cucca and Tacchi, 2012). The fair distribution and access to resources and services thus constitutes a key aspect of accessible cities and is covered in more detail in Chapter Four (Parnell, this volume).

Just as local distributional issues or strategic rationales may obstruct equitable access, it is important to hear all voices in urban developments. Citizens must be able to voice concerns, and have access to policy making, planning and decision making. This requires responsive and accountable local institutions and forms of citizen participation and engagement that go beyond periodic local elections.

Access in terms of power and justice is often particularly challenging in cities in the global South. At the household level, access through transport will be mediated through cost as well as speed and proximity to transport hubs. Where the cost of travel is prohibitive, families may come up with household strategies that prioritise travel by one or two members. This often discriminates by gender and other factors, leading to only certain members of society gaining access to earning opportunities, education and leisure that tend to be mediated by mobility. In Colombia and elsewhere, these geographical limitations may even apply to whole communities, potentially leading to social exclusion as well (Dávila, 2013).

Furthermore, inadequate infrastructure, diminishing access to basic services and livelihood opportunities are increasingly precipitating social exclusion in cities. These issues can be exacerbated by a policy shift from social welfare to liberal economies. For example in Tanzania, where this has occurred, with the exception of access to education and health services, 'cities are poorly performing in terms of access to water supply, income versus cost of living, employment, services to the handicapped and ownership of properties by sex' (Lupala, 2014, 350). Issues of power and justice can therefore hinder or ensure accessibility across geographical areas of a city, race, gender, requiring inclusive governance to implement plans.

Affordable housing

In terms of housing stock, neighbourhoods with greater density and quantity of affordable housing *types* have more affordable *rental* units than low-density neighbourhoods of single-family homes (Aurand, 2010). Second, a diversity of conditions and costs for livelihoods will create attractive neighbourhoods for all, while it is possible to push or exclude people towards sprawling suburbs due to lack of appropriate housing and services (Westerink et al, 2013). There are now some positive examples of mixed income housing in European cities, where high quality design and careful management of shared spaces has been found to be important for success (see Bailey and Manzi, 2008 in Turok 2011). Finally, accessible housing is not just about housing form, as it will require service from the relevant housing association and/or local authority.

While cost potentially limits equitable transport access in the global South (see above), there is actually also an 'affordability crisis' in cities like London and New York. In the context of neoliberal urban governance, Marom and Carmon (2015) find severe housing affordability issues in both cities, as well as a shift to dependence on market provision of affordable housing and a gradual shift away from supporting lower-income residents to those on around and above median income. In this context, there are also questions around mixed income housing, that it might undo the safety net of social housing, and may act as 'state-led gentrification' leading to displacement of poor households, for example, along the Thames in London. In addition, because market-rate developments in the UK are again separating from affordable housing, there will be 'micro-geographies of segregation' – where apparent wider neighbourhood diversity actually conceals the hyper-segregation of rich and poor. The challenge of addressing affordable housing in accessible cities is therefore far from simple.

Socio-cultural dimensions

Accessibility applies both 'internally' in terms of movement, social organisation or areas of residence and externally. Many cities are experiencing in-migration of large numbers of people from other parts of the country and internationally. On the one hand, this presents great opportunity in terms of industry and labour force. On the other, recent migrants to a city are often the most vulnerable, lacking adequate assets and resources and hence living in squalid conditions and without proper access to services or a political voice (Adams et al, 2012). City governments therefore have significant challenges in considering these dimensions of accessibility.

These challenges are currently seen in the US, where a number of cities have stopped co-operating with the federal immigration system, refusing to hand over immigrants detained by local police on account of the resource costs and because this activity is perceived to be at odds with policies trying to accommodate immigrants and ensure that they have access to city services (Badger, 2014). The mayor of Baltimore, Maryland (US), moreover, implemented a 'New Americans Task Force', and through public–private partnership developed a sustainable plan to support and retain immigrants. The programme focuses on economic growth including workforce development, small business development and housing and community wellbeing including welcome and diversity, safety and youth (Rawlings-Blake, 2014).

Ecological and public spaces

Access to ecological and public spaces is very important for cities. While most sections of this chapter cover more 'process-oriented' dimensions of accessibility (for example, proximity or means of accessing places or services), here I address a large array of public goods vital for urbanites' wellbeing to complement coverage in Chapter Three (Simon, this volume).

The World Bank describes public spaces as 'not a "nice to have" but a basic need for cities', breaking down their benefits into economic, social and environmental values (Sangmoo, 2015; see also Häkkinen et al, 2012). Moreover, research suggests that public spaces are most critical to the wellbeing of the poor, as well as the development of their communities since they do not have personal domestic space. Public spaces therefore comprise a crucial element of accessible cities and should be considered a basic service alongside transport, water and sanitation and so on.

Many factors affecting access to public and green spaces are common to general accessibility, namely proximity and 'friction of space' or transportation. Other physical accessibility factors are important too, however, such as the degree to which public space is dispersed, the availability of convenient access points and how integrated it is in urban design. Visual access becomes important for public spaces, that is, being visible from a distance and up close, while perceptions of safety also determine levels of use. Meanwhile street type is an effective factor in terms of how social interaction and the linking of private and public spaces are facilitated or retarded (Pasaogullari and Doratli, 2004).

Given the particular significance of public and green spaces for the wellbeing of the poor, it is important to note that often there is less access in contexts of higher deprivation (Lotfi and Koohsari, 2009). Examples such as Medellín, Colombia, however, show how creating public spaces and promoting connectivity can significantly improve the environment of the urban poor. The 'Metrocables' system helped to connect high-density areas of the city but, crucially, was implemented alongside social urbanism projects and an effort by the city to create physical spaces within which diverse groups could interact (Dávila, 2013). The interaction between public spaces and accessible transport is therefore a powerful tool for addressing urban poverty.

Innovation and business

Accessible cities also allow individuals the ability to access economic opportunities as well as the technology for non-physical access to cities. First, it has been shown that physical interaction fosters knowledge creation by making labour forces and greater market areas more accessible. In fact, physical infrastructure, spatial accessibility and the ability of firms to form networks are mutually reinforcing (Bentlage et al, 2013). The type of innovation this allows for creates the conditions for a 'within-urban evolution' from manufacturing towards service provision (World Bank, 2009, p.57). By considering these interactions, cities will be able to foster innovation and business.

Second, if cities are to adopt 'smart growth' models, access to technology is essential. There is currently a rapid and widespread – but spatially uneven – diffusion of information technologies that increases the connectivity of urban networks, but trying to understand or measure this phenomenon requires considerable data and resources (De Montis and Reggiani, 2013). Furthermore, one has to consider that technology-centric governance can further exclude people at the margins of power, challenging one of the dimensions of accessibility above (Simon, Chapter Three, this volume). ICTs and the Internet are not equally spread, resulting in concentrated economic development in areas of digital infrastructure, affecting competitiveness at both the macro and micro level (Tranos et al, 2013). As with physical transport, therefore, increased access to technology may well promote wellbeing for urban citizens, but also has the potential to increase inequalities.

Accessibility and urban form – what does accessibility add?

The dimensions of accessibility very much link with aspects of urban density, but they also address shortfalls of the urban density arguments and add novelty for urban development. It is certainly possible to generate accessibility through density. High density directly increases proximity to places and services and increases the likelihood of frequent transport. Further, having urban elements such as mixed land use and density will have a positive impact on access and usage of local services and facilities, as evidenced from Kuala Lumpur and Putrajaya (Rani and Mardiah, 2012). Transit-oriented development patterns increase access through proximity to transport hubs. In fact, accessibility will be influenced by interactions between land-use structure and transportation – hence a combination of density and access dimensions (Cheng et al, 2013). However, density may reduce accessibility too, for example, where higher densities are negatively correlated with housing affordability (Boyko and Cooper, 2011).

Therefore, accessibility directly addresses nuances of urban development such as power and justice and the integration of digital technologies in the urban form. While there are overlaps in place-based and transport aspects of accessibility, the concept brings new dimensions that contribute to sustainable development. The specific contributions of accessibility are as follows:

1. First, unlike density, accessibility has a normative focus, as its definition focuses on individuals achieving not just access to places but to jobs, opportunities and services and thereby increasing wellbeing. There is a distinct overlap with much of the social sustainability discourse including procedural aspects, although the framing is somewhat different.
2. Transport is a key component of accessible cities, encompassing the notion of 'access by velocity' and the ways in which different transport forms contribute to this, as well as over urban accessibility pathways. It cross-cuts different urban development patterns in this way.
3. Accessibility also strongly encompasses social dimensions, given that social systems are critical for urban renewal and sustainability. It reflects that *who* gains access is important, therefore incorporating (procedural) dimensions of power and justice.
4. Related to this, accessibility is determined by individuals' assets and social networks and so accessible cities explicitly consider equity concerns and the marginalised, specifically those geographically and socially excluded. Certain aspects of this will be focused on intra-city challenges such as affordable housing while others will

focus on creating the conditions for those moving into the city to contribute to it.

5. Accessible cities embrace digital access and create the conditions for innovation.

Future research agenda

While this chapter makes the case for accessible cities, urban density is still a useful measure and indicator in some regards. Due to the multi-dimensional nature of density described earlier, better indicators are needed that capture these different elements, especially in overcrowded and data-poor areas. Given the trade-offs described here, research is required to better understand the tensions between economic and environmental objectives and nuances within the social dimension. We need greater understanding of how urban form influences people's attachment to an area and their preference for trade-offs among living space, public facilities and proximity to jobs and services. Finally greater information is required on the extent and condition of under-used land, whether derelict/brownfield, sprawl areas, or speculative buildings (Turok, 2011).

Similarly it remains unclear whether there will be trade-offs between dimensions of urban accessibility. In order to achieve maximum benefits in implementing urban accessibility, the relationship between general accessibility and access to green space, for instance, requires further study. To achieve access to technology or rapid transport without exacerbating inequality, studies should focus on the justice impacts of these developments. As observed in Medellín, Colombia, synergies between poverty reduction and accessibility are possible and these synergies should be explored further too.

For density, most of the evidence still comes from the global North, while accessibility dimensions around power and justice, affordable housing and the status of transport development differ greatly across the global South. Comparative research in different contexts will therefore be crucial for understanding how accessible cities may evolve and reach positive trajectories. Moreover, research into accessible cities needs to consider 'planetary urbanisation', including new forms of urbanisation that are challenging conceptions of the urban as 'a fixed, bounded and universally generalizable settlement type' (Brenner and Schmid, 2011; 2014; 2015, 151). In order to consider all dimensions of accessibility, the categories, methods and cartographies that capture urban life should also be reconsidered (Brenner and Schmid, 2014).

Finally the goals for accessible cities should be seen alongside those for fair and green cities. There will be distinct overlaps for dimensions such as public and green space (with green cities) and power and justice (fair cities), while dimensions such as social infrastructure will feed into both. Ultimately, to achieve holistic sustainable urbanism, the dimensions of accessible, green and fair cities all need to be considered alongside one another, contextualised, and also assessed for synergies and trade-offs. Only through applying such a systems perspective can the maximum progress for urban dwellers' wellbeing be achieved.

Note

[1] Ecological modernisation refers to an optimistic school of thought that the economy benefits in the pursuit of environmentalism. As well as being a policy strategy and environmental discourse (Hajer, 1996), the approach focuses on increasing energy and resource efficiency while getting product and process innovations through environmental management, clean technologies and other design features. It is criticised for not challenging the real drivers behind environmental degradation or addressing environmental injustices, among others (see also Simon, Chapter Three, this volume).

References

Adams, H., Adger, N., Bennett, S., Deshingkar, P., Sward, J. and Waters, J. (2012) 'Impact of migration on urban destination areas in context of climate change', Paper commissioned by Foresight, UK Government Office for Science as a contribution to European Commission policy reflection on climate change and migration, http://migratingoutofpoverty.dfid.gov.uk/files/file.php?name=foresight-mgec-paper---ec-development-imapcts.pdf&site=354

Adger, W.N. (2003) 'Social capital, collective action, and adaptation to climate change', *Economic Geography*, 79(4): 387–404.

Alexander, D. and Tomalty, R. (2002) 'Smart growth and sustainable development: Challenges, solutions and policy directions', *Local Environment*, 7(4): 397–409.

Alexander, E. (1993) 'Density measures: A review and analysis', *Journal of Architectural and Planning Research*, 10(3): 181–202.

Angel, S., Sheppard, S.C. and Civco, D.L. (2005) *The dynamics of global urban expansion*, Washington, DC: Transport and Urban Development Department, The World Bank.

Angel, S., Parent, J., Civco, D.L. and Blei, A.M. (2011) *Making room for a planet of cities*, Cambridge: Lincoln Institute of Land Policy.

Aquino, F.L. and Gainza, X. (2014) 'Understanding density in an uneven city, Santiago de Chile: Implications for social and environmental sustainability', *Sustainability*, 6(9): 5876–97.

Aurand, A. (2010) 'Density, housing types and mixed land use: Smart tools for affordable housing?', *Urban Studies*, 47(5): 1015–36.

Badger, E. (2014) 'Why more and more cities are refusing to help the government deport immigrants', *The Washington Post*, www.washingtonpost.com/news/wonkblog/wp/2014/10/08/why-more-and-more-cities-are-refusing-to-help-the-government-deport-immigrants/

Bailey, N. and Manzi, T. (2008) *Developing and sustaining mixed tenure housing developments*, York: Joseph Rowntree Foundation.

Barter, P. (2002) 'Transport dilemmas in dense urban areas: Examples from Eastern Asia', in R. Burgess and M. Jenks (eds) *Compact cities: Sustainable urban forms for developing countries*, London and New York: Routledge, pp 271–84.

Batty, M., Axhausen, K.W., Giannotti, F., Pozdnoukhov, A., Bazzani, A., Wachowicz, M., Ouzounis, G. and Portugali, Y. (2012) 'Smart cities of the future', *The European Physics Journal Special Topics*, 214(1): 481–518, doi:10.1140/epjst/e2012-01703-3

Bentlage, M., Lüthi, S. and Thierstein, A. (2013) 'Knowledge creation in German agglomerations and accessibility: An approach involving non-physical connectivity', *Cities*, 30: 47–58.

Bostrom, M. (2012) 'A missing pillar? Challenges in theorizing and practicing social sustainability: introduction to the special issue', *Sustainability: Science, Practice, and Policy*, 8(1), http://sspp.proquest. com/static_content/vol8iss1/introduction.bostrom-print.html

Boyko, C.T. and Cooper, R. (2011) 'Clarifying and re-conceptualising density', *Progress in Planning*, 76(1): 1–61.

Boyko, C.T. and Cooper, R. (2013) 'Density and decision-making: Findings from an online survey', *Sustainability*, 5(10): 4502–22.

Bramley, G. and Power, S. (2009) 'Urban form and social sustainability: The role of density and housing type', *Environment and Planning B: Planning and Design*, 36(1): 30–48.

Bramley, G., Dempsey, N., Power, S., Brown, C. and Watkins, D. (2009) 'Social sustainability and urban form: Evidence from five British cities', *Environment and Planning A*, 41(9): 2125–42.

Brenner, N. and Schmid, C. (2011) 'Planetary urbanization', in M. Gandy (ed) *Urban constellations*, pp 10–13, Berlin: Jovis Publishers.

Brenner, N. and Schmid, C. (2014) 'The "urban age" in question', *International Journal of Urban and Regional Research*, 38(3): 731–55.

Brenner, N. and Schmid, C. (2015) 'Towards a new epistemology of the urban?', *City*, 19(2–3): 151–82.

Burton, E. (2000) 'The compact city: Just or just compact? A preliminary analysis', *Urban Studies*, 37(11): 1969–2006.

Caragliu, A., Bo, C.D. and Nijkamp, P. (2011) 'Smart cities in Europe', *Journal of Urban Technology*, 18(2): 65–82, doi:10.1080/10630732. 2011.601117

Cervero, R. (2005) *Accessible cities and regions: A framework for sustainable transport and urbanism in the 21st century*, Berkeley, CA: University of California, Berkeley Center for Future Urban Transport: A Volvo Center of Excellence, University of California, Berkeley.

Cheng, J., Bertolini, L., le Clercq, F. and Kapoen, L. (2013) 'Understanding urban networks: Comparing a node-, a density- and an accessibility-based view', *Cities*, 31: 165–76.

Churchman, A. (1999) 'Disentangling the concept of density', *Journal of Planning Literature*, 13(4): 389–411.

Churchman, A. and Ginsberg, Y. (1984) 'The image and experience of high rise housing in Israel', *Journal of Environmental Psychology*, 4(1): 27–41.

City of Cape Town (2012) *Cape Town densification policy: Technical report*, Cape Town: City of Cape Town, www.capetown.gov.za/en/Planningportal/Documents/DensificationPolicy%20web.pdf

Couclelis, H. (2000) 'From sustainable transportation to sustainable accessibility: Can we avoid a new tragedy of the commons?', in D.G. Janelle and D.C. Hodge (eds) *Information, place and cyberspace, issues in accessibility*, pp 341–56, Berlin: Springer.

Couclelis, H. and Getis, A. (2000) 'Conceptualizing and measuring accessibility within physical and virtual spaces', in D.G. Janelle and D.C. Hodge (eds) *Information, place and cyberspace, issues in accessibility*, pp 15–20, Berlin: Springer.

Criqui, L. (2015) 'Infrastructure urbanism: Roadmaps for servicing unplanned urbanisation in emerging cities', *Habitat International*, 47: 93–102.

Cucca, R. and Tacchi, E.M. (2012) 'Tradeoffs and entanglements among sustainability dimensions: The case of accessibility as a missing pillar of sustainable mobility policies in Italy', *Sustainability: Science, practice, and policy*, 8(1), http://sspp.proquest.com/archives/vol8iss1/1009-045.cucca.html

Dave, S. (2010) 'High urban densities in developing countries: A sustainable solution?', *Built Environment*, 36(1): 9–27.

Dávila, J. (ed) (2013) *Urban mobility and poverty: Lessons from Medellín and Soacha, Colombia*, London: Development Planning Unit, UCL and Universidad Nacional de Colombia, http://discovery.ucl.ac.uk/1366633/

De Montis, A. and Reggiani, A. (2013) 'Cities special section on "Analysis and planning of urban settlements: The role of accessibility"', *Cities*, 30(1): 1–3.

Dempsey, N., Bramley, G., Power, S. and Brown, C. (2011) 'The social dimension of sustainable development: Defining urban social sustainability', *Sustainable Development*, 19(5): 289–300.

Dempsey, N., Brown, C. and Bramley, G. (2012) 'The key to sustainable urban development in UK cities? The influence of density on social sustainability', *Progress in Planning* 77(3): 89–141.

Dovey, K. and Pafka, E. (2014) 'The urban density assemblage: Modelling multiple measures', *Urban Design International*, 19(1): 66–76.

Echenique, M.H., Hargreaves, A.J., Mitchell, G. and Namdeo, A. (2012) 'Growing cities sustainably', *Journal of the American Planning Association*, 78(2): 121–37.

EEA (European Environment Agency) (2006) 'Urban sprawl in Europe: The ignored challenge', *EEA Report* 10/2006, Copenhagen: EEA, www.eea.europa.eu/publications/eea_report_2006_10

Fang, K. (2015) 'Public transport and urban design', *Transport for Development*, http://blogs.worldbank.org/transport/public-transport-and-urban-design

Field, A., Witten, K., Robinson, E. and Pledger, M. (2004) 'Who gets to what? Access to community resources in two New Zealand cities', *Urban Policy and Research*, 22(2): 189–205.

Garmendia, M., Ribalaygua, C. and Ureña, J.M. (2012) 'High speed rail: Implication for cities', *Cities*, 29(2): S26–S31.

Giffinger, R., Fertner, C., Kramar, H., Kalasek, R., Pichler-Milanović, N. and Meijers, E. (2007) *Smart cities: Ranking of European medium-sized cities*, Vienna: Centre of Regional Science (SRF), Vienna University of Technology, www.smart-cities.eu/download/smart_cities_final_report.pdf

Hajer, M. (1996) 'Ecological modernisation as cultural politics', in S. Lash, B. Szerszynski and B. Wynne (eds) *Risk, environment and modernity: Towards a new ecology*, London: Sage, pp 246–69.

Häkkinen, A., Kaasalainen, H., Laitlinen, V., Nollet, C., Sagizbaeva, O., Sannemann, C. and Vuorinen, S. (2012) *Attractive shared spaces for social and environmental interaction*, Centre for Environmental: Urban Ecosystem Services.

Hansen, W. (1959) 'How accessibility shapes land use', *Journal of the American Institute of Planners*, 25(2): 73–6.

Haugen, K. (2012) *The accessibility paradox: Everyday geographies of proximity, distance and mobility*, Doctoral thesis, http://umu.diva-portal.org/smash/get/diva2:467428/FULLTEXT01.pdf

Haugen, K. and Vilhelmson, B. (2013) 'The divergent role of spatial access: The changing supply and location of service amenities and service travel distance in Sweden', *Transportation Research Part A: Policy and Practice*, 49: 10–20.

Holman, N., Mace, A., Paccoud, A. and Sundaresan, J. (2015) 'Coordinating density: Working through conviction, suspicion and pragmatism', *Progress in Planning* 101: 1–38.

Huchzermeyer, M. (2011) *Cities with 'slums': From informal settlement eradication to a right to the city in Africa*, Cape Town: University of Cape Town Press.

Iacono, M., Krizek, K.J. and El-Geneidy, A. (2010) 'Measuring non-motorized accessibility: Issues, alternatives, and execution', *Journal of Transport Geography* 18(1): 133–40.

IPCC (Intergovernmental Panel on Climate Change) (2014) *Climate change 2014: Mitigation of climate change – Transport*, Working Group III: Mitigation of Climate Change, Potsdam: IPCC.

Jiao, J., Wang, J., Jin, F. and Dunford, M. (2014) 'Impacts on accessibility of China's present and future HSR network', *Journal of Transport Geography*, 40: 123–32.

Knudsen, B., Florida, R., Gates, G. and Stolarick, K. (2007) *Urban density, creativity and innovation*, May, Creative Class Group, www.creativeclass.com/rfcgdb/articles/Urban_Density_Creativity_and_Innovation.pdf

Laguna, J. (2014) 'Institutional politics, power constellations, and urban social sustainability: A comparative-historical analysis', *Electronic Theses, Treatises and Dissertations*, http://diginole.lib.fsu.edu/islandora/object/fsu%3A254454

Lee, J., Kurisu, K., An, K. and Hanaki, K. (2015) 'Development of the compact city index and its application to Japanese cities', *Urban Studies*, 52(6): 1054–70.

Lin, J.-J. and Yang, A.-T. (2006) 'Does the compact-city paradigm foster sustainability? An empirical study in Taiwan', *Environment and Planning B: Planning and Design*, 33(3): 365–80.

Lotfi, S. and Koohsari, M.J. (2009) 'Measuring objective accessibility to neighborhood facilities in the city. A case study: Zone 6 in Tehran, Iran', *Cities*, 26(3): 133–40.

LSE (2006) *Density: A debate about the best way to house a growing population*, London: LSE, www.lse.ac.uk/geographyAndEnvironment/research/london/events/HEIF/HEIF1_05-06/density%20debate/Home.aspx

Lupala, J.M. (2014) 'The social dimension of sustainable development: Social inclusion in Tanzania's urban centres', *Current Urban Studies*, 2(4): 350–60.

Marom, N. and Carmon, N. (2015) 'Affordable housing plans in London and New York: Between marketplace and social mix', *Housing Studies*, www.tandfonline.com/doi/full/10.1080/02673037.2015.1121214

Meiring, G.H. (2013) *An exploration of the role of social systems in urban renewal: An urban planning perspective / Gert Hendrik Meiring*, Thesis. North-West University, http://dspace.nwu.ac.za/handle/10394/10216

Monzón, A., Ortega, E. and López, E. (2013) 'Efficiency and spatial equity impacts of high-speed rail extensions in urban areas', *Cities, Special Section: Analysis and Planning of Urban Settlements: The Role of Accessibility* 30: 18–30, doi:10.1016/j.cities.2011.11.002

Morris, J.M., Dumble, P.L. and Wigan, M.R. (1979) 'Accessibility indicators for transport planning', *Transportation Research Part A: General* 13(2): 91–109.

Neutens, T., Versichele, M. and Schwanen, T. (2010) 'Arranging place and time: A GIS toolkit to assess person-based accessibility of urban opportunities', *Applied Geography*, 30(4): 561–75.

Newman, P. and Kenworthy, J. (1999) *Cities and automobile dependence: An international sourcebook*, Aldershot UK: Gower.

O'Toole, R. (2001) *The folly of smart-growth*, Rochester, NY: Social Science Research Network, http://papers.ssrn.com/abstract=291805

OECD (2010) *Trends in urbanisation and urban policies in OECD countries: What lessons for China?*, Paris: China Development Research Foundation, OECD.

Pafka, E. (2013) 'Nothing gained by only counting dwellings per hectare: A hundred years of confusing urban densities', in *State of Australian Cities Conference*, Sydney.

Parnell, S. and Simon, D. (2014) 'National urbanisation and urban strategies: Necessary but absent policy instruments in Africa', in S. Parnell and E.A. Pieterse (eds) *Africa's urban revolution*, London and New York: Zed Books, pp 237–56.

Pasaogullari, N. and Doratli, N. (2004) 'Measuring accessibility and utilization of public spaces in Famagusta', *Cities*, 21(3): 225–32.

Perdue, N.A. (2013) 'The vertical space problem', *Cartographic Perspectives*, 74: 9–28.

Pierson, J. (2003) *Tackling social exclusion*, London and New York: Routledge.

Power, A. and Burdett, R. (1999) *Towards an urban renaissance*, Wetherby: Urban task force, Department of the Environment, Transport and the Regions, www.waterstones.com/waterstonesweb/advancedSearch.do?buttonClicked=2&isbn=185112165X

Rani, W.M. and Mardiah, W.N. (2012) *Modelling the relationship between urban form and social sustainability in Malaysian cities: Access to local services and public facilities*, Thesis, Edinburgh: Heriot-Watt University, www.ros.hw.ac.uk/handle/10399/2541

Rawlings-Blake, S. (2014) *The role of immigrants in growing Baltimore: Recommendations to retain and attract New Americans*, Baltimore, MD: Mayor's Office of Immigrant and Multicultural Affairs http://mayor.baltimorecity.gov/sites/default/files/RoleOfImmigrantsInGrowingBaltimore20140917.pdf

Reggiani, A. (2012) 'Accessibility, connectivity and resilience in complex networks', in K.T. Geurs, K.J. Krizek and A. Reggiani (eds) *Accessibility analysis and transport planning*, Cheltenham: Edward Elgar Publishing, pp 15–36.

Richardson, H.W. (1972) 'Optimality in city size, systems of cities and urban policy: A sceptic's view', *Urban Studies*, 9(1): 29–48.

Rode, P., Floater, G., Thomopoulos, N., Docherty, J., Schwinger, P., Mahendra, A. and Fang, W. (2014) *Accessibility in cities: Transport and urban form*, London: LSE Cities, The London School of Economics and Political Science, http://lsecities.net/publications/reports/the-new-climate-economy-report/?/

Sangmoo, K. (2015) 'Public spaces – not a 'nice to have' but a basic need for cities', *End Poverty in South Asia*, Washington, DC: World Bank, http://blogs.worldbank.org/endpovertyinsouthasia/public-spaces-not-nice-have-basic-need-cities

Satterthwaite, D. (2010) 'The role of cities in sustainable development', *Sustainable Development Insights*, 4, Boston, MA: Boston University.

Schäffler, A. and Swilling, M. (2013) 'Valuing green infrastructure in an urban environment under pressure: The Johannesburg case', *Ecological Economics*, 86: 246–57.

Schmidt-Thomé, K., Haybatollahi, M., Kyttä, M. and Korpi, J. (2013) 'The prospects for urban densification: A place-based study', *Environmental Research Letters*, 8(2): 025020.

Searle, G. and Filion, P. (2011) 'Planning context and urban intensification outcomes Sydney versus Toronto', *Urban Studies*, 48(7): 1419–38.

Sellers, J., Han, S.S., Huang, J., Lu, X.X., Marcotullio, P. and Ramachandra, T.V. (2009) 'Peri-urban development and environmental sustainability: Exampes from China and India', *Asia-Pacific Network for Global Change Research*, http://www.apn-gcr.org/resources/items/show/1556

Simon, D. (2011) 'Situating slums: Discourse, scale and place, special section, Beyond the return of the "slum"', *City*, 15(6): 674–85.

Simon, D., Arfvidsson, H., Anand, G., Bazaaz, A., Fenna, G., Foster, K., Jain, G., Hansson, S., Marix Evans, L., Moodley, N., Nyambuga, C., Oloko, M., Chandi Ombara, D., Patel, Z., Perry, B., Primo, N., Revi, A., van Niekerk, B., Wharton, A. and Wright, C. (2016) 'Developing and testing the Urban Sustainable Development Goal's targets and indicators: A five-city study', *Environment and Urbanization*, 28(1): 49–63.

Sorensen, A., Okata, J. and Fujii, S. (2010) 'Urban renaissance as intensification: Building regulation and the rescaling of place governance in Tokyo's high-rise Manshon Boom', *Urban Studies*, 47(3): 556–83.

Thinh, N.X., Arlt, G., Heber, B., Hennersdorf, J. and Lehmann, I. (2002) 'Evaluation of urban land-use structures with a view to sustainable development', *Environmental Impact Assessment Review*, 22(5): 475–92.

Tranos, E., Reggiani, A. and Nijkamp, P. (2013) 'Accessibility of cities in the digital economy', *Cities*, 30(1): 59–67.

Troy, P. (ed) (1996) *The perils of urban consolidation*, Sydney: Federation.

Turok, I. (2011) 'Deconstructing density: Strategic dilemmas confronting the post-apartheid city', *Cities*, 28(5): 470–7.

UN-HABITAT (2012) *Urban planning for city leaders*, Nairobi: UN HABITAT, www.unhabitat.org/pmss/getElectronicVersion.aspx?nr=3385&alt=1

UN-HABITAT (2013) *Planning and design for sustainable urban mobility: Global report on human settlements 2013*, New York: United Nations Humans Settlements Programme.

Vallance, S., Perkins, H.C. and Dixon, J.E. (2011) 'What is social sustainability? A clarification of concepts', *Geoforum*, 42(3): 342–8.

van Vliet, W. (1985) 'The role of housing type, household density, and neighborhood density in peer interaction and social adjustment', in J.F. Wohlwill and W. van Vliet (eds) *Habitats for children: The impacts of density*, Mahwah, NJ: Lawrence Erlbaum Associates.

Vasconcelos, A.S. and Farias, T.L. (2012) 'Evaluation of urban accessibility indicators based on internal and external environmental costs', *Transportation Research Part D: Transport and Environment*, 17(6): 433–41.

Waters, J. (2013) *The role of ecosystem services and adaptive capacity in the resilience of poor urban areas*, Norwich: University of East Anglia.

Watson, V. (2003) 'Conflicting rationalities: Implications for planning theory and ethics', *Planning Theory and Practice*, 4(4): 395–407.

Watson, V. (2009) 'Seeing from the South: Refocusing urban planning on the globe's central urban issues', *Urban Studies*, 46(11): 2259–75.

Watson, V. (2014) 'The case for a Southern perspective in planning theory', *International Journal of E-Planning Research*, 3(1): 23–37.

Weibull, J. (1976) 'An axiomatic approach to the measurement of accessibility', *Regional Science and Urban Economics*, 6: 357–79.

Weingaertner, C. and Moberg, Å. (2014) 'Exploring social sustainability: Learning from perspectives on urban development and companies and products', *Sustainable Development*, 22(29): 122–33.

Westerink, J., Haase, D., Bauer, A., Ravetz, J., Jarrige, F. and Aalbers, C.B.E.M. (2013) 'Dealing with sustainability trade-offs of the compact city in peri-urban planning across European city regions', *European Planning Studies*, 21(4): 473–97.

Whitehead, C. (2008) *The density debate: A personal view*, London: East Thames Housing Group.

Woodcraft, S. (2015) 'Understanding and measuring social sustainability', *Journal of Urban Regeneration and Renewal*, 8(2): 133–44.

World Bank and the Development Research Center of the State Council, PR China (2014) *Urban China: Toward efficient, inclusive, and sustainable urbanization*, Washington, DC: World Bank, License: Creative Commons Attribution CC BY 3.0, doi: 10.1596/978-1-4648-0206-5

World Bank (2009) *World development report 2009: Reshaping economic geography*, Washington, DC: World Bank, http://web.worldbank. org/WBSITE/EXTERNAL/EXTDEC/EXTRESEARCH/EX WDRS/0,,contentMDK:23080183~pagePK:478093~piPK:4776 27~theSitePK:477624,00.html

Ye, H., He, X., Song, Y., Li, X., Zhang, G., Lin, T. and Xiao, L. (2015) 'A sustainable urban form: The challenges of compactness from the viewpoint of energy consumption and carbon emission', *Energy and Buildings*, 93: 90–8.

Zhang, J. (2014) *Density redefined: Integrating justice into urban planning*, AAAS meeting coverage, Berkeley, CA: National Association of Science writers, www.nasw.org/article/density-redefined-integrating-justice-urban-planning

GREEN CITIES: FROM TOKENISM TO INCREMENTALISM AND TRANSFORMATION

David Simon

Introduction

This chapter examines how sustainability and green discourses and agendas relating to urban and peri-urban areas have arisen, evolved and been applied over time and in different socio-spatial contexts. It commences with a brief historical overview of the importance of health and wellbeing to the rise and embedding of urban planning as a discipline, and how early visionary efforts focused on green or public open space and garden cities. These have remained important planning foci but have been reinterpreted with changing times.

Initiatives to enhance urban sustainability through urban greening can be traced back to the 1980s, although its widespread emergence in discourse and practice is more recent. The diversity of meanings and associations attached to urban greening – indicative of its appeal in numerous contexts – is examined. Various 'weak' or instrumental approaches to urban greening can be distinguished from 'strong' versions that imply more fundamental transitions and transformations. There are strong links to climate change issues (for example, Bicknell et al, 2009; UNEP, 2012; Castán Broto and Bulkeley, 2013; UN-HABITAT, 2013; Bulkeley et al, 2014; Hodson and Marvin, 2014). Moreover, the imperative of addressing climate change is a key driver behind the recent popularisation of city greening initiatives. Conventional thinking has bifurcated climate change actions into tackling mitigation versus promoting adaptation. Recent evidence shows that this is an artificial division and that carefully targeted interventions can achieve both and also provide health and other co-benefits. Paradoxically, too, a portfolio of individually modest and incremental interventions can have aggregate effects where the whole becomes more than the sum of the parts and hence has important transformative value.

Conversely, grand high-tech 'eco-city' and smart city schemes, which have gained prominence internationally over recent years and which, rather like the phallic symbolism of tall buildings and towers, appear to have become the subject of keen competition among national and city leaders in the BRICS (Brazil, Russia, India, China and South Africa) and other dynamic regions, may prove elitist and of limited replicability and longer-term sustainability.

Historical perspectives and current resonances

Reflecting the dominance of the global North in conventional histories of urban design and planning, there is a common misperception that concerns with urban sustainability and quality of life are a recent phenomenon. In fact, however, these have far longer and more diverse histories, dating back to many ancient and precolonial cultures and mirroring the history of urbanisation as a whole. Many sophisticated and often large-scale preindustrial urban societies endured for many centuries precisely because they 'designed nature in' and lived in environmentally relatively sustainable ways. Indeed, it is increasingly being appreciated that contemporary urban sustainability challenges can learn much from how earlier urbanisms evolved, survived and eventually collapsed (for example, Douglas, 2013; Elmqvist et al, 2013a;

Simon and Adam-Bradford, 2016). Nagendra (2016) provides a highly distinctive green biography of Bengaluru (Bangalore) in Karnataka, India, tracing the changing socio-cultural attitudes to and uses and abuses of nature in the city through its 2,500-year history.

Spurred by the harmful effects of the industrial revolution on human health and the wellbeing of many factory workers and urban residents exposed to the widespread pollution, concerns about the need for open and recreational space have been central to urban planning since its emergence in the latter part of the nineteenth century. High-density living in conditions of poverty and pollution with often harsh working conditions, long hours and poor access to services triggered campaigns for improved working and living conditions and access to social services. Underpinning these were not only welfarist concerns for the workers and their families but growing recognition that such conditions threatened public health and wellbeing. The link between physical and lived environments and both household and public wellbeing was recognised and addressed in diverse ways, from opening previously royal and other parks in urban areas to the public, the popularisation of sports such as football (soccer) and the construction of playing fields for schools and clubs, and the inclusion of outdoor pursuits such a hiking and camping in the curricula of youth clubs such as Scouts and Guides.

Within emergent town planning, key innovations included land use zoning to separate residential from often polluted industrial or commercial areas and the provision of public open space for recreation (including protection for remaining common land such as village greens in the UK, which had originated as communal grazing areas). In one of the first exercises in urban master planning, Georges-Eugene (Baron) Haussmann used boulevards, parks and fountains as central elements of his comprehensive redesign of medieval Paris under Napoléon III between 1853 and 1870. Mostly hidden but equally important elements of the scheme were water supply and sewer systems. In addition to health, welfare and beautification, an important objective was urban control of often unruly mobs: linked to the new railway stations, the boulevards served as rapid deployment routes for the army and police.

Early British industrial philanthropists developed model villages such as Bourneville (Birmingham), Port Sunlight (Wirral peninsula) and Saltaire (Shipley, West Yorkshire) for their workers in the 1880s to demonstrate the possibilities and ultimately to establish the principle that workforce and community health and wellbeing were not inimical to capitalist enterprise. On the contrary, they translated into reduced absenteeism and higher productivity (and hence profit) as well as greater satisfaction and social cohesion. This link between public welfare and private profit has been central to the rationale for much urban planning in capitalist systems. Such initiatives influenced urban local authority planning regulations and found subsequent expression in, for instance, the vision of Ebenezer Howard (1898, 1902), which inspired the development of Letchworth Garden City in 1909 and Welwyn Garden City in 1920 (both in Hertfordshire, England). He spearheaded the garden city movement although his ideas were often misinterpreted, including by his planner, Raymond Unwin (see Hall, 1996, 87–135; also Friedmann, 1987).

These concerns about individual and public welfare spread internationally with the formalisation and codification of urban planning (or town and country planning as it is often still called in the UK and some parts of the British Commonwealth, and city and regional planning in the USA). For instance, Le Corbusier led the design of Chandigarh and Brasilia, the new capital cities of Punjab state in India and of Brazil respectively, while the garden city movement became international, providing an inspiration for new national and state capital cities such as Canberra in Australia and Lusaka in Northern Rhodesia (now Zambia). Bengaluru (Bangalore) was also once known as the Garden City of India, thanks in part to British influence (Nagendra, 2016). The concept also influenced the design of new towns (a broader category, not synonymous with garden cities) in the USA, Germany, outside the major British conurbations after the Second World War and elsewhere (Collins, 1969; 1980; Sutcliffe, 1981; Hall, 1996; Prakash 2002). Probably more common than entire new cities on this model, however, was to design new leafy urban expansions as 'garden suburbs' along the same principles – albeit very much catering to middle-class residents. Good examples are Hampstead Garden Suburb in London, dating from 1907, Ullevål in Oslo, built between 1916 and 1920 (Brown and Luccarelli, 2013) and Pinelands on the then outskirts of Cape Town, the first such planned suburb in South Africa and built from 1920 according to Howard's principles by a purposely established Garden Cities Trust.

The UK's Town and Country Planning Association (TCPA), one of that country's two principal professional planning associations, emerged out of the Garden Cities Association (later renamed the Garden Cities and Town Planning Association) established by Ebenezer Howard (Schuyler, 2002). It campaigns for improvements to the country's planning system and – consistent with Howard's vision – regards health, the environment, social justice and sustainable development as central pillars of its agenda, which includes a new, twenty-first century set of garden cities to tackle the UK's current urban challenges (TCPA, 2016; Wikipedia, 2016). Accordingly, the TCPA has updated its definition and key characteristics of garden cities to embrace current terminology and priorities, including the need for mixed housing:

A garden city is a holistically planned new settlement which enhances the natural environment and offers high-quality affordable housing and locally accessible work in beautiful, healthy and sociable communities. The garden city principles are an indivisible and interlocking framework for their delivery, and include:

- land value capture for the benefit of the community
- strong vision, leadership and community engagement
- community ownership of land and long-term stewardship of assets
- mixed-tenure homes and housing types that are genuinely affordable
- a wide range of local jobs in the garden city within easy commuting distance of homes
- beautifully and imaginatively designed homes with gardens, combining the best of town and country to

create healthy communities, and including opportunities to grow food

- development that enhances the natural environment, providing a comprehensive green infrastructure network and net biodiversity gains, and that uses zero-carbon and energy-positive technology to ensure climate resilience
- strong cultural, recreational and shopping facilities in walkable, vibrant, sociable neighbourhoods
- integrated and accessible transport systems, with walking, cycling and public transport designed to be the most attractive forms of local transport (TCPA, 2016).

This formulation avoids some criticisms that garden cities were essentially a romantic, European middle-class vision. Moreover, these principles are very close to those of many current green city visions internationally, as will become clear later. Related initiatives arising out of the experience of Letchworth and other garden cities include a New Garden City Movement (Ross and Cabannes, 2014). The durability of this vision, and its very close association with the notion of green space in cities – derived from the colour of grass and most temperate zone vegetation – is evident. Over a century after the establishment of Letchworth, Howard's legacy therefore remains strongly evident in the UK and beyond, rather like those of Haussmann and other visionary urban planning figures such as Le Corbusier and Frank Lloyd Wright (Friedmann, 1987; Hall, 1996; Schuyler, 2002; Parnell, Chapter Four, this volume). Some garden city principles have inspired or been incorporated in other forms and genres of new town and individual suburban design around the world.

Linking sustainability discourses to practical urban greening interventions

The evolution of urban planning is just one strand of the complex web comprising today's urban sustainability discourses and interventions. This section addresses other recent strands originating in global sustainability debates but which have become urbanised over recent decades and which provide important counterpoints to the predominantly western lineage of urban planning precepts, even when modified to suit different conditions elsewhere.

Green vs brown agendas

This first strand reflects a profound challenge from the global South sustainable development debates in terms of equity and justice in relation to perceived priorities. In essence, efforts to broaden support for wildlife and environmental conservation initiatives and National Parks in the face of increasing poaching and encroachment on conservation land for settlement, resource collection and grazing, have faced sustained critique as being elite colonial and middle-class postcolonial projects irrelevant to the needs of the poor majority. Indeed, local residents were generally evicted from such areas upon establishment, with little regard for their land and cultural rights or livelihoods – the so-called 'fortress conservation approach' (Brockington, 2002; Whitehead, 2007; Adams, 2008). The focus on iconic endangered or potentially endangered species and their habitats sent indigenous people the clear message that these animals were more important to the powers that be than local people. In urban contexts, the focus was traditionally on aesthetics and appropriate green leisure spaces, often with a heavy bias in expenditure and effort towards central (downtown) areas (Plate 3.1) and middle- and high-income residential areas (Plate 3.2). Only fairly recently, in the face of such criticisms and the need to engage local populations in conservation efforts and to promote environmental justice (see Parnell, Chapter Four, this volume), have initiatives sought to broaden participation in natural resource conservation and locally appropriate sustainability interventions (Plate 3.3). Whereas the former is known as the green agenda, the latter is known as the brown agenda, a reference to digging up the earth for housing construction and infrastructural installation in order to improve access to basic needs often still lacking in rural areas. In some assessments, the green agenda barely features at all (for example, Rojas, 2009).

Plate 3.1: Classic urban greening – 'the city beautiful' – in downtown Vancouver, Canada (Photo © David Simon)

Plate 3.2: The humid tropics facilitate natural urban greenness, although often blended with well-maintained gardens, as here in a hillside high income area of Kampala, Uganda (Photo © David Simon)

Plate 3.3: Even in the humid tropics, high density, low income areas often lack the greenery of high income areas, with exposed brown earth reflecting a lack of investment and maintained public spaces, and sometimes also livestock grazing pressure. The multi-purpose value of trees, like this one planted as part of an action research project in peri-urban Kumasi, Ghana, is therefore high (Photo © David Simon)

Even urban public spaces were implemented and maintained with a strong bias towards central districts and low density middle–class and elite residential areas (Waters, Chapter Two, this volume) and in keeping with the aspirations of such residents. Increasing housing and infrastructural backlogs for the urban poor and concern with urban sustainability and security have refocused attention on the brown agenda in terms of upgrading of low-income areas and reducing intra-urban inequalities, not least in terms of service provision, socio–spatial equity and justice (Parnell, Chapter Four, this volume). Bridging or integrating the brown and green agendas can be challenging but is achievable since they do have shared concerns with intergenerational equity and sustainable resource utilisation. Good examples include water supply and waste management at different scales (Table 3.1)

Table 3.1: Comparison of the green and brown agendas with respect to urban solid waste management.

		LOCAL LEVEL	SUB-NATIONAL LEVEL	NATIONAL LEVEL	GLOBAL LEVEL
BROWN AGENDA	CONCERNS	-health impacts -inadequate collection and disposal -livelihoods protection	-water and soil pollution -jurisdictional conflicts	-inappropriate policies	-intragenerational equity
	ACTIONS	-improve collection, and sanitary disposal -community partnerships -capacity building -cost recovery -health education	-economies of scale -landfill incineration -public-private partnerships -cost recovery	-monitoring -appropriate technology -coordinate initiatives	-awareness raising -resourcing -appropriate technology
GREEN AGENDA	CONCERNS	-wasteful lifestyles -lack of awareness -ecological & health risks	-inappropriate technology use -lack of commitment -"Not in my backyard" attitude	-wasteful production & consumption patterns -environmental degradation -inappropriate technology use	-international transfer of toxic waste -limited 'sink' capacity & finite resources -intergenerational equity
	ACTIONS	-waste reduction -recycling & reusing material -education & training	-industrial waste reduction -innovative technology & maintenance -interjurisdictional task forces -capacity building	-institutional awareness -supporting policies -green taxes & auditing -polluter pays principle -precautionary principle -economic evaluation	-advocacy campaigns & raising awareness -change in production & consumption patterns -precautionary principle

Source: modified after Allen et al, 2002, Figure 2.3, p 36.

and the numerous co-benefits of urban and peri-urban agriculture in terms of urban greening, rainfall run-off interception, and providing important subsistence and often also commercial livelihoods and health through physical activity and improved diets (Plate 3.4) (Allen et al, 2002, 35–8; Bolnick et al, 2006, 26–34; Simon, 2013; Lwasa et al, 2015; James and O'Neill, 2016).

Plate 3.4: Intensive peri-urban agriculture, Lagos, Nigeria (Photo © David Simon)

One innovative programme seeking to integrate green and brown agendas in a few progressive cities is to refocus away from simply the provision of individual parks (islands of biodiversity) and recreation areas in different areas to the importance of city-scale metropolitan open space systems (MOSS). Such integrated networks of linked open spaces of varying conservation value and intensity of human use constitute important biodiversity corridors while providing multiple co-benefits including ecosystem services such as shade, moisture retention in the soil and hence runoff mitigation services – as will be discussed later in this chapter – and leisure areas. Inevitably, pressure on land for alternative uses, coupled with rising land values (the so-called 'urban premium') constitutes a major challenge to establishing and maintaining the integrity of such corridors and networks (Roberts et al, 2012).

Strong vs weak sustainability

One little discussed but vital dimension of sustainability discourses, and which does have direct urban implications, is the distinction between weak and strong sustainability. As sustainability gained international prominence and popularity in the wake of the Brundtland Commission's (WCED, 1987) report, it soon lost traction through use and abuse in a wide diversity of contexts. At one extreme were the so-called 'greenwash' approaches, which were sometimes little more than cynical appropriations of the term to provide a cloak of acceptability over 'business as usual' approaches including unsustainable practices by companies or other bodies. More common are various 'weak' sustainability approaches that share the characteristics of promoting modest or incremental reforms. While positive in their own terms, such interventions do not tackle any of the forces, drivers or underlying power relations of unsustainability. Actions which do attempt the latter are termed 'strong' sustainability approaches (Simon, 2003; 2016). This distinction applies equally well to economic and urban greening approaches. Examples of 'weak' sustainability and greening include fitting low energy light bulbs, switching off street lights in non-essential areas during the early hours of the morning and recycling waste to save resources, including energy, and reduce landfill. 'Strong' examples include development of accessible, reliable and affordable integrated public transport services for an urban area, linked to pedestrianisation schemes and reduced parking to reduce reliance on private motor vehicles and encourage walking and recreational use of street space.

Discourses and practices of economic greening

As previously with sustainability, economic greening has been adopted or appropriated in multiple discourses, with the associated implications for change ranging from the superficial and incremental to the profound. Key distinguishing features are how substantial the tensions or trade-offs between economic growth/development and environmental sustainability are held to be, and how they could be addressed. This constitutes 'an uneasy balance' in the words of Bina's (2013) subtitle. At one extreme, the tensions are regarded as minimal and the likely changes therefore mainly cosmetic or incremental (see ecological modernisation below). At the other extreme, perspectives like ecological Marxism hold that the underlying contradictions within capitalist relations of production are so profound that resolution is impossible. As Brockington and Ponte (2015, 2198) express it succinctly, 'Behind the Green Economy lies a bundle of paradoxes and contradictions. The term is both a rallying call for radical change to the organisation of economic activity and social life, and an instrument by which meaningful alterations of either is resisted.' Of course, green economic discourses are developed and promoted by stakeholders seeking to articulate and defend or challenge divergent and often conflicting interests. Dominant discourses seek to legitimise marketised neoliberal strategies as unproblematic in promoting sustainability (Perrot, 2015; Scoones et al, 2015).

Death (2015) discerns four principal paradigms of economic greening propagated by major multilateral agencies and as manifested in the national green economic development programmes of the BRICS and some other countries, namely green growth, green resilience, green transformation and green revolution. He focuses on national strategies in the global South in order to broaden critical engagement beyond the OECD countries and to counteract the principally rural and case-study nature of existing literature:

> there is an absence of serious consideration of the national strategies and developmental programmes being deployed by

Third World states, some of which are mobilising the green economy in ways which have only peripheral relationships to the traditionally 'green' issue areas of conservation and natural resource management. (Death, 2015, 2208)

He traces the recent rapid explosion of green economic discourses to the economic recession since 2008, and the stimulus of the United Nations Environment Programme's (UNEP's) (2009; 2011) programmatic advocacy and, like Simon (2016), he points to antecedents as far back as the 1980s when sustainability discourses first dominated world headlines and environmental economics gained ascendancy. However, as Simon (2016) and this chapter demonstrate in contrast to Death's contention, economic greening is not entirely a state-centric policy discourse but has strong subnational and especially urban components too. It is important to note, moreover, that these latter have not always followed from national initiatives but have frequently preceded and even contributed to the formulation of national policies. In large part, this reflects a different path to greening trodden by progressive urban local authorities. Tackling climate change adaptation and mitigation challenges has become a leading urban priority since most of the climate change drivers and many of its impacts pose serious threats to vulnerable urban areas and communities. As will become clear below, ecosystems services and urban greening strategies are seen as important elements in such strategies.

Death's (2014) paper assessed South Africa's green economic policy context in relation to his discursive typology, finding elements of all four discourses present. Swilling et al (2016) concur with this assessment by Death but favour a hybrid approach of green structural transformation *with growth* which they, in common with many other commentators and political leaders, see as essential in the context of the crucial challenges of addressing high un- and underemployment in the global South. This approach amounts to sustainability-oriented just transitions (Swilling et al, 2016: xxviii–xxxvii). Expressed thus, the links between greening and the other two key attributes of fair and sustainable societies addressed in this book, namely accessibility and fairness, are self-evident. This applies equally at the urban scale, as set out in the chapters on fair and accessible cities (Parnell, Chapter Four, and Waters, Chapter Two, this volume) and will be elaborated upon below. Socio-ecological perspectives and regimes, such as the ecosystem services approach, are important in urban arenas and will also be discussed below rather than here. Myers (2016) provides a substantive analysis of urban environmental politics in African contexts.

One other important discourse is that of *ecological modernisation*, which – although a diffuse approach – is closely linked to neoliberalism and involves market-driven valuation and use of environmental resources (for example, Hajer, 1995; Murphy, 2000) in a manner consistent with 'weak' sustainability as summarised earlier. It can be applied at different geographical scales, including the urban arena and informs strategies to value ecosystem services as policy tools (see below).

Disaster risk reduction (DRR) and climate change approaches

These two approaches had different origins but have coalesced increasingly over recent years to the point where most participants regard them as overlapping but distinct perspectives rather than climate change being a special case of disaster risk as DRR specialists initially argued (Simon, 2012). DRR has evolved over some 30 to 40 years from concerns to reduce the impact and cost of natural and then also anthropogenic disasters, to prediction and where possible prevention or at least minimising the risk, hazard and scale of likely disasters when they strike (Wisner et al, 2012; Adelekan et al, 2015). In terms of translating concepts into policy and practical interventions, the area of overlap between the two approaches, around reducing vulnerabilities and promoting resilience to various forms of hazard and disaster, including climatic and broader environmental extreme events and more incremental changes to prevailing conditions, has rightly become a principal focus.

The field of climate or broader global environmental change is vast and complex, having expanded dramatically over the last quarter century or so from its initial base within climatology and related natural sciences. It has become the quintessential interdisciplinary and indeed also transdisciplinary field, with social scientific and non-academic research inputs increasingly important. Climate change has two distinct elements, namely the increasing severity and possibly now also frequency of extreme events (wherein lies the overlap with disaster risk), and the slow-onset changes to underlying or prevailing conditions, such as sea level rise. Both have direct salience in the context of urban areas, not least because of ongoing urbanisation processes and increasing concentrations of economic activity there. Recognition of this at the highest levels is reflected, for instance, in the inclusion for the first time in the Intergovernmental Panel on Climate Change's (IPCC's) Fourth Assessment Report (AR4) of explicit urban coverage, which was further enhanced to an entire chapter in AR5 (IPCC, 2007; 2014).

The storms of controversy surrounding the vocal climate sceptic lobby, which have bedevilled political discourse, challenged the credibility of the IPCC and inhibited progress in many arenas, and often sharpened divergent perspectives among stakeholder groups (Adger et al, 2009; Giddens, 2009; Helm and Hepburn, 2009; Hulme, 2009; Matthew et al, 2010; Bond, 2012) have subsided in the last few years in the face of the increasing weight of evidence. As with sustainability and related discourses, social, technical and (human) security dimensions of greening, DRR and climate change are becoming more important (for example, Matthew et al, 2010; Sygna et al, 2013). One approach gaining increasing attention in this context is ecosystem-based adaptation (EbA), explicitly bringing ecological principles and ecosystem conservation together with climate change adaptation; it may be linked to community-based adaptation (CBA), which may be a fruitful way forward in urban contexts. The severity of the challenges is now generally acknowledged, although the diverse ideological currents remain evident, even in relation to the urban arena.

While DRR and climate change policies and programmes can and do operate at all scales, the most specific actions are often appropriate to the ecosystem and local scales, usually as a responsibility of local authorities, including in urban areas. Very much for this reason, urban local governments have become increasingly active in this regard, either independently or as part of multi-level governance and financial support arrangements or from other sources. Recent attention to the challenges facing cities in poorer regions has increased markedly in recent years as the urgency of taking action and prioritising interventions in resource-scarce contexts has become more evident. Such analyses and policy agendas are increasingly focusing on the potential contributions of restored and conserved ecosystem services, including 'soft engineering' and diverse forms of urban greening within integrated strategies to reduce vulnerability, enhance resilience and promote urban transformation (for example, Birkmann and von Teichman, 2010; Carmin et al, 2012; Cartwright et al, 2012; UNEP, 2012; Bulkeley and Tuts, 2013; Silver et al, 2013; Simon, 2013; 2016; Birkmann et al, 2014; Friend et al, 2014; Kernaghan and da Silva, 2014; Adelekan et al, 2015; Cartwright, 2015; Lindley et al, 2015; Simon and Leck, 2015). One particular socio-technical approach to addressing these related urban sustainability challenges is represented by eco-cities, smart cities and smart grids (see below).

It is crucial to note that such socio-technical and market-oriented approaches, including *ecological modernisation* and the valuation of ecosystem services, are not neutral since market forces produce and reproduce differentiation, including of spatial, economic, social and environmental vulnerabilities at all scales, including urban and intra-urban. Such structural vulnerabilities also constitute a form of unfairness or injustice (see Parnell, Chapter Four, this volume). Hence an understanding of these forces and of vulnerability as an outcome of such processes rather than as being merely coincidental or 'just how it is', is essential to the formulation of appropriate amelioration or transformative policies and programmes (see Dooling and Simon (2012) for elaboration and US case studies).

Greening cities: making sense of the mantra

Given the diversity of ideological and pragmatic influences underlying the plethora of urban greening discourses and initiatives, it is often not possible to trace direct or straightforward linkages since particular programmes or interventions frequently derive from multiple influences and pathways. These include:

- requirements or incentives to comply with policy agendas 'from above' in the form of regional and/or national government institutions, international agencies and/or donors;
- agreed actions formulated or emulated 'horizontally' within international city networks such as the C40 and its Climate Leadership Group; international agencies and associations like United Cities and Local Governments (UCLG), Local Authorities for Sustainability (ICLEI) and the Commonwealth Local Government Forum, or national groupings; and
- internal processes and priorities, among which the role of individual institutional champions is often crucial (Leck and Roberts, 2015).

Accordingly, against the conceptual background of the previous sections, the remainder of this chapter examines and seeks to explain the diverse urban interventions evident around the world by means of several intersecting typologies. Even the terms 'green cities' and 'green urbanism' – which are sometimes used as synonyms – have no standard definitions and are used heterogeneously. Green urbanism is sometimes distinguished from ecological modernisation by virtue of having ecology at its heart rather than merely using it instrumentally (Luccarelli and Røe, 2013b, 4–7), but this usage is not widespread.

One analytical lens is viewing cities as socio-economic, socio-technical and/or socio-ecological systems, within each of which greening can play particular roles. Within *the socio-economic approach,* emphasis falls on the economic value of greening, tending towards the instrumental perspective in terms of which new infrastructural investment, economic activities, technologies and employment opportunities are created. There is increasing evidence from diverse contexts that sustained urban economic greening can produce a significant *net* employment gain, with new 'green jobs' exceeding losses through decline in obsolete, polluting industries (UNEP, 2012; Simon 2013; 2016; UN-HABITAT, 2013).

The socio-economic approach accords most closely with neoliberal and mixed economic paradigms, including, for instance, 'climate-crisis capitalism' (Bond, 2012) and superficial greenwashing to provide a progressive veneer over conventional and even unsustainable practices. However, it also includes many interventions contributing to important sustainability and lifestyle (and health) improvements, such as insulation of buildings, new low- or zero-carbon construction technologies and systems, and expansion of urban and peri-urban agriculture (UPA) as a means of providing both employment and enhanced local food supply and security (James and O'Neill, 2016). Many of these initiatives will be referred to below in greater detail.

The socio-technical approach is particularly appropriate to assessing district- or citywide interventions where technical innovation permits comprehensive redesign or new constructions to produce apparently new, technologically and environmentally greener and more sustainable visions and urban fabrics. Several such waves of so-called eco-cities and smart cities can be discerned over the last decade or more. These have been accompanied on the one hand by extensive and high-profile promotion by the transnational corporate interests behind their design, financing and construction, and on the other by competition among city and national leaders – most conspicuously at present, the Indian Prime Minister, Narendra Modi – to demonstrate their green and modernist credentials. Inevitably, such schemes therefore frequently become highly politicised and contested, both in political and also local activist terms (Datta, 2012; 2014; 2015; UN-HABITAT, 2013; Söderström, et al, 2014; Bunnell, 2015; Greenfield, 2015; Harris, 2015; Jazeel, 2015).

Luque et al (2014) set out a helpful set of critical questions for interrogating smart grids, smart cities and more locally grounded alternatives, in terms of the main pressures and drivers, the social interests promoting them, the vision and rebundling of infrastructures, the social organisation underlying them, the spatial priorities, and emerging consequences. However, they do not consider environmental, sustainability or green dimensions, which are no less important. Overall, despite presentational distinctiveness, the substantive differences among the various mainstream prototypes appear relatively modest and they share the vision of utilising new advanced low-carbon and 'smart' information and communications, transport and construction technologies to build clean, low-energy and highly integrated work and living environments.

In almost all cases, fundraising and construction have lagged years behind schedule because of the financial crisis, the scale of investment required, technical challenges and/or political uncertainties. Moreover, the entire vision and orientation of these utopian imaginaries are towards elite and middle-class careers, workspaces and lifestyles, putting them beyond the realms of widespread replicability and irrelevant to the needs, affordability and priorities of the urban poor, who form the majority of urban dwellers in most rapidly growing urban contexts. Indeed, they often erase local histories, ecologies and poor communities cleared to make way for the new construction, hence generating strong local opposition and injustice (see Parnell, Chapter Four, this volume). There are also concerns about the implications of smart technological grids for authoritarian control and surveillance.

Smart and eco-cities both reflect and contribute to the culture of modernist and capitalist emulation that already drives the rampant and inappropriate replication of unsustainable western urban designs and private car ownership for the incipient and new middle classes in rapidly urbanising regions. The extent to which these elite utopian visions offer substantive pathways to alternative and genuinely sustainable urban futures – including replacing conventional private cars with high degrees of integrated and grid-controlled public transport – remains highly dubious; some would even suggest this to be an oxymoron (Meinhold, 2009; Chang and Sheppard, 2013; Cugurullo, 2013; Shwayri, 2013; Kennedy et al, 2014; Hodson and Marvin, 2010; 2014; Datta, 2012; 2014; 2015; Söderström et al, 2014; Greenfield, 2015; Jazeel, 2015; Simon and Leck, 2015; Watson, 2015; Waters, Chapter Two, this volume). Bunnell's recent critique poses two pertinent questions:

To what extent are newly politicised terrains giving rise to imaginings and narratives of smart(er) futures that incorporate ideals of social justice? And, in what ways can investment in smart technology-enabled futures yield returns to more than just the corporate interests and political elites behind the smart cities business model in India? (Bunnell, 2015, 48)

To these concerns about social injustice and narrow controlling interests, as with Luque et al's (2014) schema, we must add the need to demonstrate substantial contributions to urban sustainability and greenness, not just visually and aesthetically appealing living and working environments for the urban elite.

The socio- (or social) ecological perspective is most widely applied in terms of the natural systems and resource flows in and through urban areas. Extreme 'deep ecological' approaches and even organismic analogies proffered by some commentators do not have much purchase in urban contexts on account of their quintessentially anthropogenic and open character, being parts of wider systems. Far more useful is therefore to consider 'urban nature' or natural elements within towns and cities, what roles they play, how adequate and sustainable they are, and what strategies could be adopted to enhance their integrity and value. Urban areas of all sizes and types depend on air, water, open spaces and vegetation of certain minimum standards. In the course of industrial-style economic development, however, such resources have been undervalued and often destroyed and degraded to the point of triggering urban health crises from air and water pollution, unsanitary conditions as a result of inadequate sewerage, drainage and water supply systems or lack of fitness as a result of loss of public open space for recreation. Such crises formed the basis for the garden cities movement and other utopian urban model towns, as discussed in the Introduction to this chapter, and which sought to provide healthy, wholesome and, in today's terms, sustainable urban living environments.

The recent sub-disciplines of environmental and ecological economics and urban ecology have contributed greatly to enhanced understanding of, and attempts to value, urban natural resources.

Reflecting the holistic approach, the recent focus on green infrastructure and open space systems is now beginning to be broadened to green–blue agendas integrating terrestrial and aquatic resources and spaces. What these perspectives share is a concern to demonstrate the importance of well-functioning urban nutrient and other cycles and hence to imbue them with positive value for planners and decision-makers as well as ordinary residents, not least in relation to DRR and ecosystem-based climate change mitigation and adaptation (Plate 3.5). Although often challenging, this is seen as the best way to argue for their conservation, enhancement and expansion (for example, Ten Brink, 2011; Gómez-Baggethun and Barton, 2013; Van Zoest and Hopman, 2014; Elmqvist et al, 2015; Lindley et al, 2015; Luederitz et al, 2015).

Plate 3.5: Conservation of ground cover on steep slopes and of some vegetation in and around informal settlements maintains slope stability, intercepts storm run-off and improves soil penetration by rainwater. These valuable ecosystem services are vital for poor and wealthy alike, as here in peri-urban Durban, South Africa, in the context of extreme events and climate change (Photo © David Simon)

Sometimes attempts to quantify the benefits in terms of assigning cardinal monetary values to particular resources so as to include them in cost–benefit analysis, other multi-criteria decision-making tools or as the basis for well-intentioned programmes of payment for ecosystem services (PES) have gone too far, leading to distortions or perverse results. This can occur when the most easily measured variables or services are included and others excluded or assigned conservative estimated values, or where – as in unequal multicultural urban and peri-urban contexts – such valuations reflect the priorities and values of dominant or professional groups but which conflict sharply with those of marginalised or subordinate groups. The overall net benefits of PES are also coming increasingly into question (Le Velly and Dutilly, 2016). More extreme critiques regard such quantification merely as evidence of the pervasiveness of capitalism and the subordination of nature to it. Conversely, considerable effort has gone into designing and implementing pro-poor PES schemes by development agencies and NGOs, albeit overwhelmingly in rural rather than urban contexts (for example, Forest Trends et al, 2008; GEF, 2014).

Overall, understanding of urban ecology and associated biodiversity issues and challenges in different agro-ecosystemic and climatic contexts has increased rapidly over recent years (for example, Alberti, 2009; Newman et al, 2009; Müller et al, 2010; Richter and Weiland, 2012; Elmqvist et al, 2013b, 2016; Marcus and Colding, 2014). Accordingly, examining ecosystem services has become the most widely used analytical tool, seeking to assess the nature and importance of the 'services' that nature provides to people, in this case in urban areas. Four categories can be distinguished: *supporting* (for example, sources of water, photosynthesis and homes to living species), *provisioning* (such as supply of air, water and soil nutrients, urban agriculture), *regulatory* (for example, carbon sequestration, water filtering, storm surge interception) and *cultural* (recreational, spiritual and symbolic spaces and resources – the last mentioned often associated with rivers, lakes and hills or other topographical features in indigenous cultures). These categories are not discrete and the respective ecosystem services may take place simultaneously and in complementary ways (Cilliers et al,

2013; Elmqvist et al, 2013b). Colding and Barthel (2013) demonstrate the diverse benefits of the 'urban green commons' in Detroit, USA, a classic post-industrial 'rust belt' city.

Ultimately, ecosystem maintenance and enhancement are seen as the basis for building resilience in socio/social-ecological systems. At least seven interrelated principles for achieving this have recently been elaborated: maintaining species and habitat diversity and redundancy, managing connectivity among the elements; managing slow variables and feedbacks; fostering complex adaptive systems thinking; broadening participation among all relevant stakeholder groups; promoting polycentric (that is, decentralised or devolved) governance (Biggs et al, 2015). Surprisingly, these authors barely mention urban areas but the principles also apply in such contexts, albeit often in different forms and even more complex participatory and governance arrangements.

Meeting the challenges of climate change mitigation and adaptation, and urban sustainability more generally, has greatly stimulated interest in and research on the social-ecological approach and especially the role of ecosystem services. This links directly to urban greening initiatives, especially in view of evidence that restoration of natural filters and barriers, such as estuaries, coastal mangrove swamps and river margins, and eroded hillsides and slopes is often more effective at mitigating the impact of extreme events and changes to prevailing conditions than hard engineering structures. The latter tend to deflect or displace the problem downstream, often to more vulnerable low-lying areas and communities. Increasing the extent and quality of vegetative ground cover also enhances urban biodiversity and encourages the return or growth of other species, and has other co-benefits in terms of health and senses of wellbeing (Romero Lankao et al, 2012; Trundle and McEvoy, 2016; see Figure 3.1), enhanced leisure spaces and opportunities and urban food production (as discussed earlier). This also helps to reduce urban heat island effects, which is an important form of climate change mitigation.

Until very recently, the geographies of research on and implementation of these approaches have been heavily skewed towards OECD

Figure 3.1: Schematic representation of relationships between urban greening and human physical activity levels.

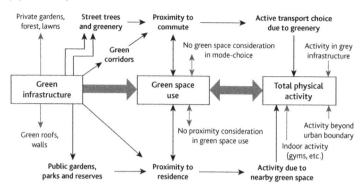

Source: Modified after Trundle and McEvoy, 2016, Figure 19.3, p 281.

countries, reflecting the origins of such work and understanding of its potential. Breaking this mould, the volume on urban biodiversity and ecosystem services by Elmqvist et al (2013b) includes city-level assessments of Chicago, New York, Melbourne, Stockholm, Istanbul, Cape Town and Rio de Janeiro. Within Africa, there has been little application outside South Africa's metropolitan cities (Cilliers et al, 2013).

Finally, but not least in this regard, it is apposite to mention the increasing importance of the close relationships between urban environments, comprising both the built and natural components, and human security. Human security discourses have only recently started to become urbanised, emphasising and demonstrating the environmental security aspects of urban greening in terms of mitigating climate change and other extreme events, enhanced urban agriculture in terms of local food supply and security, and the calming effects that access to green open space, shaded and attractive areas have in relation to social tension and urban unrest. As mentioned above, however, intra-urban variations in (in-)security reflect underlying politico–economic processes and social differentiation, including unemployment rates, which often impose constraints on the extent of transformative policy in practice (for example, Hodson and Marvin, 2009; Simon and Leck, 2010; Sygna et al, 2013; Waters, Chapter Two, this volume).

Urban greening initiatives: the importance of spatial scale

There are several possible ways to classify the diverse range of initiatives beneath the umbrella of urban greening. Complementing and cross cutting the conceptually and programmatically organised approaches surveyed so far, this section presents, with specific examples, a typology based on geographical scale, organised from smallest to largest.

The typology commences with *individual buildings* (new and retrofitting/upgrading) and households. This is the lowest decision-making scale and the lowest at which initiatives can be undertaken. Although it is often believed that individual actions at this level are insignificant relative to the scale of intervention required, their importance lies both in the value of the demonstration effect to neighbours and friends and in terms of the aggregate effect of large numbers of individual actions. Examples include fitting low-energy light bulbs and solar (photovoltaic) panels; retrofitting loft or wall insulation and double glazing where not already installed; recycling household waste where possible and composting organic waste; installing green walls and roofs (Plate 3.6); walking or cycling for short journeys; using public transport where convenient and feasible rather than private vehicles; or buying hybrid or electric cars. Most such measures remain voluntary, however, albeit sometimes incentivised through subsidies – an issue returned to in the concluding section below. Most South African urban developers prefer individual new green buildings to brownfield redevelopment and retrofitting because of the perceived complexity and risks, not least relating to state policies (Seeliger and Turok, 2015).

The next level is the *street block*, at which certain economies of scale apply if residents club together to buy or install in bulk, or at which some recycling services and facilities or retrofitting actions listed above are more economically organised. The Transition Street initiative organised by the transition towns movement exemplifies this well

Plate 3.6: Green walls and balcony or roof gardens, as here in Manhattan, New York City (USA), are aesthetically attractive and important for carbon sequestration (Photo © David Simon)

(see internet resources). The third appropriate level is the *local area or suburb*, where local authorities may be persuaded to provide some strategic interventions at a larger scale, or where they become feasible, such as district heating. This is also the scale at which comprehensive redevelopment can take place, for example, when redundant factories, waterfront or riverfront wharves and warehouses, or areas of housing are demolished and remodelled for contemporary use (Plate 3.7). With such redevelopment, current local design standards must be adhered to and energy efficient and low carbon construction materials and designs should be utilised. Water efficient plumbing and grey water reuse systems can be included at scale, as well as forward looking urban designs in terms of multipurpose green infrastructure and urban biodiversity conservation and enhancement to ensure that co-benefits as outlined above are maximised. 'Climate proofing' design standards should also be included.

Plate 3.7: Green infrastructure: the Hudson River Park on Manhattan's Lower West Side, which replaced derelict wharves and warehouses, has provided valuable green shade and recreation space, and increased urban biodiversity and carbon sequestration capacity (Photo © David Simon)

At both these scales, the distinction between *greenfield* and *brownfield* (re-)development becomes highly relevant in relation to sustainability and urban greening. Greenfield refers to new construction on previously vegetated land (hence 'green'), often associated with urban expansion in or beyond the peri-urban interface and hence potentially contributing to urban sprawl and lower average urban densities, with increased per capita or per hectare costs of service provision. In terms of sustainability, priority should be given to redevelopment of brownfield land within the existing urban boundaries, that is land which has previously been built on. Such land can vary in location and scale from individual buildings to street blocks or entire areas such as obsolete or derelict harbour or river fronts, factory sites and residential estates (Plate 3.8). Because existing sewerage, water and other utilities abut such land, the costs of connection are much lower, while such redevelopment enhances residential densities and urban compactness (the opposite of sprawl) (for example, Chen et al, 2008; Waters, Chapter Two, this volume), thereby reducing per capita costs and also providing new sources of property tax revenue for the local authorities. While the majority of such comprehensive redevelopment schemes target middle-class residents, this is not always the case and they provide good opportunities to apply strong sustainability approaches that promote fairness in access to higher value, more attractive green urban environments through mixed housing provision that incorporates a percentage of affordable designs (sometimes called social housing) as well (Parnell, Chapter Four, this volume; Waters, Chapter Two, this volume). Such urban regeneration also contributes to rejuvenating run-down areas and repopulates cities from which previous generations of residents suburbanised. Urban safety and security there are also thereby enhanced.

Plate 3.8: Nanjing (People's Republic of China) exemplifies urban infrastructural greening as part of comprehensive redevelopment to tackle industrial pollution and unsustainable urbanism (Photos © David Simon)

Next, there is the *urban scale* of the entire town or city, at which the local authority or, more rarely, all the local authorities comprising a metropolitan area, can institute citywide measures on greening urban infrastructure, energy efficiency and waste recycling, although the practicability of this will depend on the balance between local and regional authority powers and responsibilities. At this scale, co-benefits of integrated planning and implementation can be substantial. This also enables local authorities to use the locally most appropriate lever(s) as justification or framing logic in order to maximise public buy-in, such as climate change (for example, Cartwright et al, 2012; City of Boulder, 2015), overt greening (for example, UNEP, 2012; Luccarelli and Røe, 2013a; Simon, 2013), economic regeneration, net employment gain or energy efficiency. Whether the city in question is economically dynamic or regenerating and hence growing, or in decline and hence shrinking or hollowing out will also determine the extent to which large-scale redevelopment and economic restructuring are possible. This would provide the opportunity (ideally requirement) to 'design in' more comprehensive large-scale green spatial organisation, renewable energy systems, low-carbon technologies and functioning urban ecosystems and biodiversity than is feasible with smaller-scale interventions. However, as a recent study of Gauteng in South Africa demonstrates, the risk of not tackling the fundamental underlying issues, and hence failing to make the transition away from urban unsustainability, is considerable (Götz and Schäffler, 2015).

Finally, the *city region* constitutes the most appropriate scale in terms of biophysical processes (for example, bio-region/agro-ecological zone, watershed/river basin) and economic activities and resource utilisation (functional region). However, since such regions generally extend well beyond the urban built-up area and municipal or metropolitan boundaries, this scale of planning or intervention is difficult to undertake unless an intermediate form of governance institution with appropriate boundaries and powers exists between local and national authorities (for example, provinces, states, counties or regions). Hence, for instance, the world's leading reporting mechanism for subnational climate change commitments explicitly includes local and regional governments (carbon*n*® Climate Registry, 2016).

Conclusions

Although they have longer histories than generally believed, urban greening and the growing impetus to encourage green and sustainable cities are very topical agendas, initially within wealthier countries but increasingly now worldwide. As the critical and systematic analysis above has demonstrated, these discourses and practical impulses have diverse theoretical and conceptual origins and implications. They can, of course, be and sometimes are exploited for private and corporate vested interest. A key public policy challenge is therefore to align private profit with public benefit as far as possible and to eliminate or at least minimise negative externalities where the public suffers negative impacts. The net employment and commercial value-added potentials of greening products, processes and interventions may prove critical factors in overcoming resistance on grounds of claimed job losses when obsolescent firms and industries are shut.

Green agendas at all scales but especially in urban areas reflect a complex mix of stimuli and objectives. Nevertheless, a key potential lies in the many examples of co-benefits that can be obtained from progressive measures, whether introduced directly to mitigate or adapt to climate change, promote public health and senses of human security or to make cities more attractive lived environments for their residents. This is important in the context of constrained public finances and implementation capacity in many local governments, and provides powerful justification for appropriate interventions.

One of the constraints to implementation of many of the changes advocated here is outdated urban planning legislation in many parts of the world. Such statutes and regulations reflect not only particular property rights and rules of access but also modernist urban planning theories and values from the mid-twentieth century that are ill-suited to the complexities and dynamics of contemporary urbanism and the practical needs of poorer urban residents. However, precisely because of the power of vested interests and institutional inertia, effecting change is both difficult and slow (Berrisford, 2014), even when the need for change to promote urban energy sustainability, urban and peri-urban agriculture and other forms of environmental greening is accepted (for example, Froestad et al, 2012; Lwasa et al, 2015). Sometimes, when legislative or regulatory change is impracticable, non-enforcement of inappropriate existing regulations can itself be an important means of de facto support, such as permitting urban and peri-urban cultivation on open public spaces.

This challenge – already alluded to in relation to minimising negative externalities – also focuses attention on *the balance between voluntarism and regulation* in respect of urban climate change and other greening interventions. In societies where private property rights are sacrosanct, many individuals deeply resent state regulation and 'interference', even in relation to societal challenges. The archetypical but by no means only example is the USA, where public sector interventions are often highly circumscribed by political acceptability, and where progressive city administrations, such as the example of Boulder, Colorado, cited above, therefore stand out. However, wherever there are democratically contested elections, popular opinion provides a barometer, sometimes restricting action but also rejecting policies seen as serving specific vested interests at the expense of others. Nevertheless, electoral politics and powerful vested interests constitute one reason why the challenge of crossing the threshold from incremental or reformist greening interventions to transformative change is likely to prove difficult.

Although environmental issues, most prominently subsumed under climate change challenges, are definitely rising up urban political agendas, only rarely have they to date become decisive election battlegrounds. Yet, even so, may local authorities worldwide have been able to introduce and enforce compliance with regulations covering significant greening measures for different categories of building and open space, ranging from insulation to recycling, energy conservation, building construction standards, permeable surfaces of patios and driveways to permit rainwater infiltration and reduce surface runoff, and control of invasive alien plant species. Equally significant are subsidies and other incentive schemes by local governments and official agencies to stimulate voluntary uptake of greening measures and those, which, while not necessarily perceived as related to greening, have this as co-benefits, like rooftop solar panel or micro-turbine installation, planting indigenous rather than exotic species, recycling grey water, use of borehole and grey water for irrigating golf courses and playing fields, use of bicycles for short commutes and leisure, car pooling and use of public transport. For many private firms, voluntary compliance with sustainability or green codes of practice and construction standards has become a matter of pride and positive promotional value. Examples include the BREEAM in the UK (the world's oldest, established in 1990 and now applied around the world), GBCSA Green Star rating in South Africa and equivalent schemes run by the Australian, Dutch, Norwegian and Swedish and many other national Green Building Councils.

One final note of caution linking socio-economic, socio-technical and social-ecological realms within the urban arena is appropriate. Implicit and to some extent explicit in discourses of city greening is the taming or domestication of nature to fit the requirements of urban design, such as conserving and rehabilitating coastal or estuarine mangrove swamps, riverbanks, other urban wetlands and terrestrial social-ecological systems. Many waterways and parklands are intensively utilised for leisure and recreation activities on lawned areas and demarcated playing fields but many others are maintained in a supposedly 'natural' state from which people are excluded. Unless some endangered or threatened species/habitat or ecosystem is the specific rationale for a conservation area, urban nature should not be divorced from human activity:

> Urban designers and landscape architects can't ignore human culture in their efforts to make environmentally innovative cities. Every attempt to turn to nature for broad brushstroke solutions is really a turn towards a particular *idea* of nature – nature as the absence of human intention, human meddling, human *design*. Yet design is inevitable, if we're talking about the design of

trees and grasses and greenery, and even the most conservative urban conservation project can never actually put things back the way they were before humans showed up. (Silva, 2016, no page number)

References

Adams, W.M. (2008) *Green development* (3rd edn), London: Routledge.

Adelekan, I., Johnson, C., Manda, M., Matyas, D., Mberu, BU., Parnell, S., Pelling, M., Satterthwaite, D. and Vivenkananda, J. (2015) 'Disaster risk and its reduction: An agenda for urban Africa', *International Development Planning Review*, 37(1): 33–43.

Adger, W.N., Lorenzen, I. and O'Brien, K. (eds) (2009) *Adapting to climate change*, Cambridge: Cambridge University Press.

Alberti, M. (2009) *Advances in urban ecology: Integrating humans and ecological processes in urban ecosystems*, New York: Springer.

Allen, A., You, N., Meijer, S., Atkinson, A., Marom, N., McAlpine, P., Nims, S., Soave, A., Walker, J., Davila, J. and Fernandes, E. (2002) *Sustainable urbanisation: Bridging the green and brown agendas*, London: Development Planning Unit, UCL.

Berrisford, S. (2014) 'The challenge of urban planning law reform in African cities', in S Parnell, E Pieterse (eds) *Africa's urban revolution*, London: Zed Books, pp 167–83.

Bicknell, J., Dodman, D. and Satterthwaite, D. (eds) (2009) *Adapting cities to climate change: Understanding and addressing the development challenges*, London: Earthscan.

Biggs, R., Schlüter, M. and Schoon, M.L. (eds) (2015) *Principles for building resilience: Sustaining ecosystem services in social-ecological systems*, Cambridge: Cambridge University Press.

Bina, O. (2013) 'The green economy and sustainable development: An uneasy balance?', *Environment and Planning C: Government and Policy*, 31: 1023–47.

Birkmann, J. and von Teichman, K. (2010) 'Integrating disaster risk reduction and climate change adaptation: Key challenges – scales, knowledge, and norms', *Sustainability Science*, 5(2): 171–84.

Birkmann, J., Garschagen, M. and Setiadi, N. (2014) 'New challenges for adaptive urban governance in highly dynamic environments: Revising planning systems and tools for adaptive and strategic planning', *Urban Climate*, 7: 115–33.

Bolnick, J., Kayuni, H.M., Mabala, R., McGranahan, G., Mitlin, D., Nkhoma, S., Oucho, J., Sabri, A., Sabry, S., Satterthwaite, D., Swilling, M., Tacoli, C., Tambulasi, R.I.C. and Van Donk, M. (2006) 'A pro-poor agenda for Africa: Clarifying ecological and development issues for poor and vulnerable populations', *Human Settlements Discussion Paper Series, Urban Change* 2, London: International Institute for Environment and Development, www.iied.org/pubs.iied.org/pdfs/10533IIED.pdf

Bond, P. (2012) *Politics of climate justice: Paralysis above, movement below*, Durban: University of KwaZulu University Press.

Brockington, D. (2002) *Fortress conservation: The preservation of the Mkomazi Game Reserve, Tanzania*, Oxford: James Currey.

Brockington, D. and Ponte, S. (2015) 'The green economy in the global South: Experiences, redistributions and resistance', *Third World Quarterly*, 36(12): 2197–206.

Brown, M. and Luccarelli, M. (2013) 'Oslo's Ullevål Garden City: An experiment in urbanism and landscape design', in M Luccarelli, PG Røe (eds) *Green Oslo: Visions, planning and discourse*, Farnham and Burlington, VT: Ashgate, pp 81–115.

Bulkeley, H. and Tuts, R. (2013) 'Understanding urban vulnerability, adaptation and resilience in the context of climate change', *Local environment: The international journal of justice and sustainability*, 18(6): 646–62.

Bulkeley, H.A., Edwards, G.A.S. and Fuller, S. (2014) 'Contesting climate justice in the city: Examining politics and practice in urban climate change experiments', *Global Environmental Change*, 25: 1–40.

Bunnell, T. (2015) Smart city returns, *Dialogues in Human Geography*, 5(1): 45–8.

carbon*n*® Climate Registry (2016) '5-Year Overview Report 2010–2015', http://e-lib.iclei.org/wp-content/uploads/2015/12/cCR2015_5Year_Report.pdf

Carmin, J., Anguelovski, I. and Roberts, D. (2012) 'Urban climate adaptation in the global south: Planning in an emerging policy domain', *Journal of Planning Education and Research*, 32: 18–32.

Cartwright, A. (2015) 'Better growth, better cities: Rethinking and redirecting urbanization in Africa', *The New Climate Economy Working Paper*, www.newclimateeconomy.net

Cartwright, A., Parnell, S., Oelofse, G. and Ward, S. (eds) (2012) *Climate change at the city scale: Impacts, mitigation and adaptation in Cape Town*, Abingdon: Routledge.

Castán Broto, V. and Bulkeley, H. (2013) 'Maintaining climate change experiments: Urban political ecology and the everyday reconfiguration of urban infrastructure', *International Journal of Urban and Regional Research*, 37(6): 1934–48.

Chang, I.-C.C. and Sheppard, E. (2013) 'China's eco-cities as variegated urban sustainability: Dongtan eco-city and Chongmin Eco-Island', *Journal of Urban Technology*, 20(1): 57–75.

Chen, H., Jia, B. and Lau, S.S.Y. (2008) 'Sustainable urban form for Chinese compact cities: Challenges of a rapid urbanized economy', *Habitat International*, 32(1): 28–40.

Cilliers, S., Cilliers, J., Lubbe, R. and Siebert, S. (2013) 'Ecosystem services of urban green spaces in African countries: Perspectives and challenges', *Urban Ecosystems*, 16(4): 681–702.

City of Boulder (2015) *Boulder's climate commitment*, Draft, October, Boulder, CO: City of Boulder, www-static.bouldercolorado.gov/docs/11-24-15_Climate_Commitment_Online_Resource-1-201603281510.pdf

Colding, J. and Barthel, S. (2013) 'The potential of 'urban green commons' in the resilience building of cities', *Ecological Economic*, 86: 156–66.

Cugurullo, F. (2013) 'How to build a sandcastle: An analysis of the genesis and development of Masdar city', *Journal of Urban Technology*, 20(1): 23–37.

Collins, J. (1969) 'Lusaka: The myth of the garden city', *Zambian Urban Studies*, 2, Lusaka: University of Zambia Institute for Social Research.

Collins, J. (1980) 'Lusaka: Urban planning in a British colony, 1931–64', in G. Cherry (ed) *Shaping an Urban World*, London: Mansell.

Datta, A. (2012) 'India's ecocity? Environment, urbanisation, and mobility in the making of Lavasa', *Environment and Planning C: Government and Policy*, 30(6): 982–96.

Datta, A. (2014) 'India's smart city craze: Big, green and doomed from the start?', *Guardian*, 17 April, www.theguardian.com/cities/2014/apr/17/india-smart-city-dholera-flood-farmers-investors

Datta, A. (2015) 'New urban utopias of postcolonial India: Entrepreneurial urbanization and the smart city in Gujarat', *Dialogues in Human Geography*, 5(1): 3–22.

Death, C. (2014) 'The green economy in South Africa: Global discourses and local politics', *Politikon*, 41(1): 1–22.

Death, C. (2015) 'Four discourses of the green economy in the global South', *Third World Quarterly*, 36(12): 2207–24.

Dooling, S. and Simon, G. (eds) (2012) *Cities, nature and development: The politics and production of urban vulnerabilities*, Farnham and Burlington, VT: Ashgate.

Douglas, I. (2013) *Cities: An environmental history*, London and New York: IB Tauris.

Elmqvist, T., Redman, C., Barthel, S. and Costanza, R. (2013a) 'History of urbanization and the missing ecology', in T. Elmqvist, M. Fragkias, J. Goodness, B. Güneralp, P.J. Marcotullio, R.I. McDonald, S. Parnell, M. Sendstad, M. Schewenius, K.C. Seto and C. Wilkinson (eds) *Urbanization, biodiversity and ecosystem services: Challenges and opportunities. A global assessment*, Dordrecht, Heidelberg, New York and London: Springer Open, pp 13–30.

Elmqvist, T., Fragkias, M., Goodness, J., Güneralp, B., Marcotullio, P.J., McDonald, R.I., Parnell, S., Sendstad, M., Schewenius, M., Seto, K.C. and Wilkinson, C. (eds) (2013b) *Urbanization, biodiversity and ecosystem services: Challenges and opportunities. A global assessment*, Dordrecht, Heidelberg, New York and London: Springer Open.

Elmqvist, T., Setälä, H., Handel, S.N., Van der Ploeg, S., Aronson, J., Blignaut, J.N., Gómez-Baggethun, E., Nowak, D.J., Kronenberg, J. and De Groot, R. (2015) 'Benefits of restoring ecosystem services in urban areas', *Current Opinion in Environmental Sustainability*, 14: 101–8.

Elmqvist, T., Zipperer, W.C. and Güneralp, B. (2016) 'Urbanization, habitat loss and biodiversity decline: Solution pathways to break the cycle', in K.C. Seto, W.D. Solecki, C.A. Griffith (eds) *The Routledge handbook of urbanization and global environmental change*, London and New York: Routledge, pp 139–51.

Forest Trends, The Katoomba Group, UNEP (United Nations Environment Programme) (2008) *Payments for ecosystem services. Getting started: A primer*, www.unep.org/pdf/PaymentsForEcosystemServices_en.pdf

Friedmann, J. (1987) *Planning in the public domain: From knowledge to action*, Princeton, NJ: Princeton University Press.

Friend, R., Jarvie, J., Reed, S.O., Sutarto, R., Thinphanga, P. and Toan, V.C. (2014) 'Mainstreaming urban climate resilience into policy and planning: Reflections from Asia', *Urban Climate*, 7: 6–19.

Froestad, J., Shearing, C., Herbstein, T. and Grimwood, S. (2012) 'City of Cape Town solar water heater by-law: Barriers to implementation', in A. Cartwright, S. Parnell, G. Oelofse, S. Ward (eds) *Climate change at the city scale: Impacts, mitigation and adaptation in Cape Town*, pp 244–62, Abingdon: Routledge.

GEF (Global Environment Facility) (2014) *GEF investments on payment for ecosystem services schemes*, Washington, DC: GEF, www.thegef.org/gef/sites/thegef.org/files/publication/28252nomarks.pdf

Giddens, A. (2009) *The politics of climate change*, Cambridge: Polity.

Gómez-Baggethun, E. and Barton, D.N. (2013) 'Classifying and valuing ecosystem services for urban planning', *Ecological Economics* 86: 235–45.

Götz, G. and Schäffler, A. (2015) 'Conundrums in implementing a green economy in the Gauteng city-region', *Current Opinion in Environmental Sustainability*, 13: 79–87.

Greenfield, A. (2015) 'Zeroville-on-Khambhat, or: The clean slate's cost', *Dialogues in Human Geography*, 5(1): 40–4.

Hajer, M. (1995) *The politics of environmental discourse: Ecological modernization and the policy process*, Oxford: Oxford University Press.

Hall, P. (1996) *Cities of tomorrow: updated edition*, Oxford: Blackwell.

Harris, A. (2015) 'Smart ventures in Modi's urban India', *Dialogues in Human Geography*, 5(1): 23–6.

Helm, D. and Hepburn, C. (eds) (2009) *The economics and politics of climate change*, Oxford: Oxford University Press.

Hodson, M. and Marvin, S. (2009) 'Urban ecological security: A new paradigm?', *International Journal of Urban and Regional Research*, 33(1): 193–215.

Hodson, M. and Marvin, S. (2010) 'Can cities shape socio-technical transitions and how would we know if they were?', *Research Policy*, 39(4): 477–85.

Hodson, M. and Marvin, S. (2014) 'Securitization of urban environments: Sustainable urbanism or premium ecological enclaves?', in M Hodson, S Marvin (eds) *After sustainable cities?*, London and New York: Routledge, pp 91–103.

Howard, E. (1898) *To-morrow: A peaceful path to real reform*, London: Swan Sonnenschein & Co (2nd edn 1902, entitled *Garden cities of tomorrow*, London: Swan Sonnenschein & Co).

Hulme, M. (2009) *Why we disagree about climate change*, Cambridge: Cambridge University Press.

IPCC (2007) *Climate Change 2007: Impacts, adaptation and vulnerability. Working Group II contribution to the Fourth Assessment Report of the IPCC*, Cambridge: Cambridge University Press.

IPCC (2014) *Climate Change 2014: Impacts, adaptation and vulnerability. Working Group II contribution to the Fifth Assessment Report of the IPCC*, Cambridge: Cambridge University Press.

James, S.W. and O'Neill, P.M. (2016) 'Planning for peri-urban agriculture: a geographically-specific, evidence-based approach from Sydney', *Australian Geographer*, 47(2): 179-194, DOI: 10.1080/00049182.2015.1130676

Jazeel, T. (2015) 'Utopian urbanism and representational city-ness: On the Dholera before Dholera smart city', *Dialogues in Human Geography*, 5(1): 27–30.

Kennedy, C., Ibrahim, N. and Hoornweg, D. (2014) 'Low-carbon infrastructure strategies for cities', *Nature Climate Change*, 4, pp 343–6, doi: 10.1038/NCLIMATE2160

Kernaghan, N. and da Silva, J. (2014) 'Initiating and sustaining action: Experiences building resilience to climate change in Asian cities', *Urban Climate*, 7: 47–63.

Leck, H. and Roberts, D. (2015) 'What lies beneath: Understanding the invisible aspects of municipal climate change governance', *Current Opinion in Environmental Sustainability*, 13: 61–7.

Le Velly, G. and Dutilly, C. (2016) 'Evaluating payments for environmental services: Methodological challenges', *PLOS One*, 11(2): 20.

Lindley, S.J., Gill, S.E., Cavan, G., Yeshitela, K., Nebebe, A., Woldegerima, T., Kibassa, D., Shemdoe, R., Renner, F., Buchta, K., Abo-el-Wafa, H., Printz, A., Sall, F., Coly, A., Ndour, N.M., Feumba, R.A., Zogning, M.O.M., Tonyé, E., Ouédraogo, Y., Samari, S.B. and Sankara, B.T. (2015) 'Green infrastructure for climate adaptation in African cities', in S. Pauleit, G. Jorgensen, S. Kabisch, P. Gasparini, S. Fohlmeister, I. Simonis, K. Yeshitela, A. Coly, S. Lindley, and W.J. Kombe (eds) *Urban vulnerability and climate change in Africa*, Dordrecht, Frankfurt and London: Springer Verlag, pp 107–52.

Luccarelli, M. and Røe, P.G. (eds) (2013a) *Green Oslo: Visions, planning and discourse*, Farnham and Burlington, VT: Ashgate.

Luccarelli, M. and Røe, P.G. (2013b) 'Introduction: Nature, urbanism and liveability', in M. Luccarelli, P.G. Røe (eds) *Green Oslo: Visions, planning and discourse*, Farnham and Burlington, VT: Ashgate, pp 1–24.

Luederitz, C., Brink, E., Gralla, F., Hermelingmeier, V., Meyer, M., Niven, L., Panzer, L., Partelow, S., Rau, A-L., Sasaki, R., Abson, D.J., Lang, D.J., Wamsler, C. and Von Wehrden, H. (2015) 'A review of urban ecosystem services: Six key challenges for future research', *Ecosystem Services*, 14: 98–112.

Luque, A., McFarlane, C. and Marvin, S. (2014) 'Smart urbanism: Cities, grids and alternatives?', in M. Hodson, S. Marvin (eds) *After sustainable cities?*, London and New York: Routledge, pp 74–90.

Lwasa, S., Mugagga, F., Wahab, B., Simon, D., Connors, J. and Griffith, C. (2015) 'A meta-analysis of urban and peri-urban agriculture and forestry in mediating climate change', *Current Opinion in Environmental Sustainability*, 13: 68–73.

Marcus, L. and Colding, J. (2014) 'Towards an integrated theory of spatial morphology and resilient urban systems', *Ecology and Society*, 19(4): 55.

Matthew, R.A., Barnett, J., McDonald, B. and O'Brien, K.L. (eds) (2010) *Global environmental change and human security*, Cambridge, MA and London: Massachusetts University Press.

Meinhold, B. (2009) Songdo IBD: South Korea's new eco-city, 4 September, http://inhabitat.com/songdo-ibd-south-koreas-new-eco-city/

Müller, N., Werner, P. and Kelsey, J.G. (eds) (2010) *Urban biodiversity and design*, Oxford: Wiley-Blackwell.

Murphy, J. (2000) 'Editorial: Ecological modernisation', *Geoforum*, 31(1): 1–8.

Myers, G. (2016) *Urban environments in Africa: A critical analysis of environmental politics*, Bristol: Policy Press.

Nagendra, H. (2016) *Nature in the city: Bengaluru in the past, present and future*, New Delhi: Oxford University Press.

Newman, P., Beatley, T. and Boyer, H. (2009) *Resilient cities: Responding to peak oil and climate change*, Washington DC: Island Press.

Perrot, R. (2015) 'The Trojan horses of global environmental and social politics', in L.K. Mytelka, V. Msimang, R. Perrot (eds) *Earth, wind and fire: Unpacking the political, economic and security implications of discourse on the green economy*, Johannesburg: Real African Publishers for Mapungubwe Institute for Strategic Reflection, pp 31–52.

Prakash, V. (2002) *Chandigarh's Le Corbusier: The struggle for modernity in postcolonial India*, Seattle, WA: University of Washington Press.

Richter, M. and Weiland, U. (eds) (2012) *Applied urban ecology: A global framework*, Chichester: Wiley-Blackwell.

Roberts, D., Boon, R., Diederichs, N., Douwes, E., Govender, N., McInnes, A. and McLean, C. (2012) 'Exploring ecosystem-based adaptation in Durban, South Africa: Learning-by-doing' at the local government coal face', *Environment and Urbanization*, 24(1): 1–29.

Rojas, E. (2009) 'El fundamento de la sostenibilidad', in E. Rojas (ed) *Construir Cuidades; Mejoramiento de barrios y calidad de vida urbana*, Washington, DC: Banco Interamericano de Desarrollo, pp 219–51.

Romero Lankao, P., Qin, H. and Dickinson, K. (2012) 'Urban vulnerability to temperature-related hazards: A meta-analysis and meta-knowledge approach', *Global Environmental Change*, 12: 670–83.

Ross, P. and Cabannes, Y. (2014) *21st century garden cities of tomorrow: A manifesto*, London: New garden city movement, www.newgardencitymovement.org.uk

Schuyler, D. (2002) *From garden city to green city: The legacy of Ebenezer Howard*, Baltimore, MD: Johns Hopkins University Press.

Scoones, I., Leach, M. and Newell, P. (eds) (2015) *The politics of green transformations*, London: Earthscan from Routledge.

Seeliger, L. and Turok, I. (2015) 'Green-sighted but city-blind: Developer attitudes to sustainable urban transformation', *Urban Forum*, 26: 321–41.

Shwayri, S.T. (2013) 'A model Korean ubiquitous eco-city: The politics of making Songdo', *Journal of Urban Technology*, 2(1): 39–55.

Silva, P. (2016) 'Sustainable cities don't need nature – they need good design', *The Nature of Cities*, www.thenatureofcities. com/2016/02/21/sustainable-cities-dont-need-nature-they-need-good-design/

Silver, J., Bulkeley, H. and Tuts, R. (eds) (2013) 'Urban vulnerability, adaptation and resilience: Analysing the lessons from UN-Habitat's CCCI, Special Issue', *Local Environment*, 18(6): 643–751.

Simon, D. (2003) 'Dilemmas of development and the environment in a globalising world: Theory, policy and praxis', *Progress in Development Studies*, 3(1): 5–41.

Simon, D. (2012) 'Hazards, risks and global climate change', in B. Wisner, I. Kelman and J.-G. Gaillard (eds) *The Routledge handbook of hazards and disaster risk reduction*, Routledge, Abingdon and New York, pp 207–19.

Simon, D. (2013) 'Climate and environmental change and the potential for greening African cities, special issue on Resurgent African Cities?', *Local Economy*, 28(2): 203–17.

Simon, D. (2016) 'The potential of the green economy in addressing urban environmental change', in K.C. Seto, W.D. Solecki, C.A. Griffith (eds) *Handbook on urbanization and global environmental change*, London and New York: Routledge, pp 455–69.

Simon, D. and Adam-Bradford, A. (2016) 'Archaeology and contemporary dynamics for more sustainable and resilient cities in the peri-urban interface', in B. Maheshwari, V.P. Singh, B. Thoradeniya (eds) *Balanced urban development: Options and strategies for liveable cities*, Water Science and Technology Library 72, Dordrecht and Heidelberg: Springer, pp 57–83.

Simon, D. and Leck, H. (2010) 'Urbanizing the global environmental change and human security agendas', *Climate and Development*, 2(3): 263–75.

Simon, D. and Leck, H. (2015) 'Understanding climate adaptation and transformation challenges in African cities', *Current Opinion in Environmental Sustainability*, 13: 109–16.

Sutcliffe, A.R. (1981) *Towards the planned city: Germany, Britain, the United States and France, 1780–1914*, Oxford: Blackwell.

Söderström, O., Paasche, T. and Klauser, F. (2014) 'Smart cities as corporate story telling', *City*, 18(3): 307–20.

Swilling, M., Musango, J.K. and Wakeford, J. (2016) 'Introduction: Deepening the green economy discourse in South Africa', in M. Swilling, J.K. Musango, J. Wakeford (eds) *Greening the South African economy: Scoping the issues, challenges and opportunities*, Cape Town: University of Cape Town Press, pp xxvii–liii.

Sygna, L., O'Brien, K. and Wolf, J. (eds) (2013) *A changing environment for human security: Transformative approaches to research, policy and action*, Abingdon and New York: Earthscan from Routledge.

TCPA (Town and Country Planning Association) (2016) *Garden city principles*, www.tcpa.org.uk

Ten Brink, P. (ed) (2011) *The economics of ecosystems and biodiversity in national and international policy making*, London: Earthscan.

Trundle, A. and McEvoy, D. (2016) 'Urban greening, human health and well-being', in K.C. Seto, W.D. Solecki, C.A. Griffith (eds) *Handbook on urbanization and global environmental change*, London and New York: Routledge, pp 276–92.

UNEP (United Nations Environment Programme) (2009) *Global green new deal*, Nairobi: UNEP.

UNEP (United Nations Environment Programme) (2011) *Towards a green economy: Pathways to sustainable development and poverty eradication*, Nairobi: UNEP.

UNEP (United Nations Environment Programme) (2012) *Sustainable, resource efficient cities – making it happen!*, Nairobi: UNEP.

UN-HABITAT (2013) *State of the World's Cities 2012/2013: Prosperity of cities*, Nairobi: UN-HABITAT.

Van Zoest, J. and Hopman, M. (2014) 'Taking the economic benefits of green space into account: the story of the Dutch TEEB for Cities project', *Urban Climate*, 7: 107–14.

Watson, V. (2015) 'The allure of 'smart city' rhetoric: India and Africa', *Dialogues in Human Geography*, 5(1): 36–9.

Whitehead, J. (2007) 'Fortress conservation and accumulation by dispossession: The case of Shoolpaneshwar Sanctuary in the Narmada Valley', in B.S. Nayak (ed) *Nationalizing crises: The political economy of public policy in contemporary India*, New Delhi: Atlantic, pp 261–82.

Wikipedia. (2016) Town and Country Planning Association, https://en.wikipedia.org/wiki/Town_and_Country_Planning_Association

Wisner, B., Kelman, I. and Gaillard, J.-G. (eds) (2012) *The Routledge handbook of hazards and disaster risk reduction*, Abingdon and New York: Routledge.

WCED (World Commission on Environment and Development) (1987) *Our common future*, New York: Oxford University Press.

4
FAIR CITIES: IMPERATIVES IN MEETING GLOBAL SUSTAINABLE DEVELOPMENTAL ASPIRATIONS

Susan Parnell

Introduction

The approval of the Sustainable Development Goals (SDGs) in 2015 marked a shift in global values, introducing the idea that people everywhere should aspire to universally applicable development aspirations that 'leave no one behind' (UN, 2015). The SDGs endorse the idea that making cities, as well as nations, work differently forms an integral part of achieving alternative, more sustainable, futures for this and subsequent generations. The hallmark of the post-2015 agenda is that it embraces a clear commitment to an integrated understanding of ecological, social and economic issues at multiple scales – including the hitherto largely ignored domain of cities. To this end the four threads of the new urban goal (Goal 11: *Make cities inclusive, safe, sustainable and resilient*) are interdependent and need to be considered as integrated aspirations, not isolated components of individual, city, national and global sustainable developmental strategies (SDSN, 2013).

Operationalising this ambitious new post-2015 vision, even in poor and unequal urban contexts, requires a commitment to the socially protective value underlying the urban SDG along with making the way people (especially rich ones) live in cities more publicly accountable and less harmful to the planet.

At the outset it is important to sketch what is meant by fairness in the urban context. Ideally being born a man or a woman, black or white, Muslim or Christian, gay or straight, able or disabled should make no difference to an individual's or community's life choices, but in contemporary cities this is rarely, if ever, the case (Plate 4.1). Similarly there is today no reason for there to be different versions of fairness for past, current and future generations of urban residents. Possibly the biggest immediate challenge implied by the post-2015 agenda is to accept that fairness needs to be calibrated in a universal way that gives African or Asian urban residents and those living in European or North American cities, for instance, exactly the same minimum rights and protections, instead of holding on to fragmented value systems that define norms and standards according to where in the world the city is located. The logic is simple – all urban lives matter equally and should be protected.

The post-2015 agenda embraces a commitment to address the ways in which cities everywhere function, in part to ensure that they enhance, not detract from, access to individual and collective wellbeing but also to enable the system of cities to function in ways that uphold the integrity of the natural systems on which life depends. Hence, global, national and city leaders are beginning to assess how they might change their practice to better align action in, on and from cities with this utopian vision of sustainable development. The universal concept of 'a fair city' provides a translational bridge between what is said and what can actually be done in the diverse urban circumstances where inequality and unfair practice prevail (Parnell and Pieterse, 2015). Integrating into a single process the conception, design and execution of an idea intended to bring about change, this chapter probes what making a fairer urban future might entail; both for thought and action in the urban domain.

Plate 4.1: Different life prospects: City traders, London; second-hand clothing vendor and customers, Maputo; beggar, Copenhagen, respectively (London and Copenhagen © Susan Parnell; Maputo © David Simon)

The focus here falls on the city scale but this does not imply that everything required to realise fair urban development should be generated from or controlled by sub-national government. Rather the purpose of the city-scale emphasis adopted here is a reminder that policies and programmes designed to drive a fairer world have not hitherto been sufficiently conceived or driven by city authorities, nor generally have the requisite funds always been allocated to the sub-national scale. As a result, cities are not only the locus of unequal wages and inequitable access to wealth-generating assets like land and housing, but there has been inadequate effort to minimise the impact of the elevated levels of inequality found within cities. A central purpose of the chapter is to make the case for city-scale mitigation of unfair urban form, culture and management.

The idea of a fair city is not a new or an entirely different way of seeing things – it builds on an extensive theoretical literature dealing with utopian concepts of urban welfare, the good city, the just city, the right to the city and even the resilient city – as well as a mass of policy-oriented debate around the most appropriate instruments and tools for achieving urban inclusion, redistribution and equity. In drawing these ideas together, the notion of the fair city presented here is not just a synthesis of abstract ideas or a moral position statement. This recasting of the relevance and utility of these ideas, many of them originating over a century ago, is fresh in two important respects. First it offers a deliberately Southern sensibility to reflect the location of the contemporary global epicenter of urbanism (Parnell and Oldfield, 2014), and second the value of ideas typically generated by scholars is juxtaposed, counterpointed and fused with experiences of practice. These two points of departure, ideas and action, also provide the overarching structure for the chapter.

The first section of this chapter makes the point that, given global trends in urbanisation, any universal conception of a fairer urban future has to resonate with the imperatives facing cities of the global South, or it will have little legitimacy. At the same time, the challenge of making cities fair has never been greater in places that have had traditionally strong social safety nets and good public interest protection. Such mechanisms are now under threat from neo-liberalism and the associated general decline in state capacity and systematic reduction of social protection. In many respects this has made European cities more like those of North America, where public protection was never strong. Austerity and changes in public policy in the North means some parts of rich-country cities increasingly resemble the cities of middle-income countries. This congruence is amplified because across emerging market economies, including the powerful and populous BRICS nations (Brazil, Russia, India, China and South Africa), urban social protection is on the rise (Ballard, 2013). The challenge is therefore not to think about a specific city or sub-type of urban place, but rather to take up the problem of the universal urban meaning of fairness in what is now the dominant form of human settlement.

The second section of the chapter is mindful of a common global urban future, where what happens by way of social protection in one city reverberates across the globe – not just socially but also politically, economically and ecologically. It is also informed by the recognition that the sources of knowledge required to generate radically different ways of reducing inequity, especially if they draw from established ideas, will have to be sensitive to context and to be locally legitimate and actionable. The material thus draws from reflections of an international team of urbanists (scholars and practitioners) working within a partnership known as Mistra Urban Futures (MUF) (www.mistraurbanfutures.org/en). In setting out their normative agenda, MUF were interested in understanding why and how inequality and exclusion manifests in cities. An associated (note: not secondary) concern was to probe alternative and durable modes to conceive, design, build and manage cities to ensure that the structural inequality that cities produce is ideally prevented or at least reduced and that the impacts of unfair opportunities within and between cities are mitigated.[1] In scaling up the discussion, praxis grounded in Southern realities is thus foregrounded. The global challenge is to develop new notions of how distributional or administrative justice can operate in a resource-restricted city. Ways must therefore be found to ensure that the benefits of urban design can be made or kept public rather than private in cities with weak government, in order to minimise inter- and intra-urban injustices.

The central premise of the chapter as a whole is that responding to urban inequality and injustice is not only a technical or political issue; there is also a dearth of intellectual imagination about how to make the urban future fairer. Thinking and acting proactively in the city in a normative way, that is openly committed to making things fair and correcting what is clearly unfair, opens a major site of innovation and opportunity for expanded transformative sustainable development. The city thus becomes a site of action, alongside traditional global, national and neighbourhood interventions, for ensuring fair access to wellbeing, economic opportunities and resources.

An ideal urban future (as viewed from the South)

Perceptions of what is fair, equal and/or just are related, overlapping and at times contested urban ideas and practices: for example, not everyone defines equity and justice in the same way. The point here is not to set one idea of fairness against another, but rather to begin by unlocking the importance of how we think about values in relation to the city and then to uncover the key agents and instruments that can advance such value-based interventions in the urban context.

The role of ideas in defining a fairer urban future

The relationship of urbanisation to the uneven evolution of capitalism continues to attract high-level theorisation (Harvey, 2012; Brenner, 2013), but until the global community took up the campaign for an international consensus on cities in the new sustainable development framework there was almost no attention paid to mediating experiences of fairness in the evolving unequal geography of the system of cities.[2] By contrast, the European Union consciously mediates resource distribution across cities of its member states (Faludi, 2002) and many national governments are concerned to ensure some degree of fairness between cities within their national territory and so they invoke national laws and regulations on minimum standards for urban health and safety[3] and often generate national spatial strategies to incentivise growth or bolster welfare in deprived urban regions (Healey, 2004). Where supra-national or national urbanisation policies are absent or fail, the developmental gaps between and within cities are left unchecked. The massive disparities that mark the urban experiences of residents in the north and south of the United Kingdom are an example of this within one national territory, highlighting that fairness is as much an inter-city issue as it is an intra-city issue (Massey, 1984). Acknowledging the importance of the wider regional and national spatial context of urban development, UN-HABITAT is now pushing the idea of National Urban Development Plans, through the HABITAT III preparations, as a possible means of tracking the multi-scale commitments necessary to realising SDG Goal 11 (www.habitat3. org). More generally what the SDGs and HABITAT III represent is an effort to define a global agenda for all cities, thus addressing the inter-national and intra-national discrepancies of the quality of urban life.

Leaving aside the global and national political economy of the system of cities, our focus turns to a discussion of equity, justice and fairness at the city scale.[4] The literature on the range of fiscal and institutional capacities in different parts of the world to deliver fairness in the urban context is understandably fractured, reflecting divergent political and intellectual views as well as varied geographical circumstances. Other than ideological cleavages around what should reasonably be expected of government in redistribution and social protection at the city scale, the most obvious divide is between the conception and application of notions of justice or fairness in high-, middle- and low-income contexts. Even in similar socio-economic contexts, national and cultural traditions of public policy and local politics shape what is perceived as fair and how fairness should be achieved in cities and towns. There are especially significant points of contention around how to view the role of the state and gender equity.

Debates among urban practitioners and policy makers on how to make fairer places are very well developed in the global North (Hall, 1996), with the extensive comparative urban literature on affordable housing, welfare, social inclusion and even inclusive urban design peaking in the 1990s.[5] This is not necessarily a field restricted to the centrality of national or local state action. From as early as the 1980s, however, the attention of urban planners in Europe turned away from direct delivery of social protection and the role of the state to focus on participatory planning and areas of community action, in what was termed the communicative turn (Healey, 2003). Across the largely established cities and towns of the global North, basic needs were assured (even if there was political contestation over the levels, costs and best means of delivery). The local urban governance literature thus expanded, effectively diluting the centrality of the role of urban planning and putting a stronger emphasis on issues of complex governance: both multi-party local governance and multi-scalar governance (Brenner, 1999).

In the academic effort to deal conceptually with the increasingly complex management of cities and to promote the place of civil society in running cities, the proactive role of the local political parties and the local state in securing a level urban playing field was displaced. The concern to demonstrate the injustices of neoliberalism and the elite capture of cities through processes like gentrification, securitisation and privatisation created an intellectual culture that emphasised the exposure of new forms of unfairness, rather than the practice-oriented construction of urban regimes that could promote greater fairness. Practical engagements about how to deliver minimum housing standards, how to put in place meaningful redistribution or how to foster equity in city labour markets and other nuts and bolts mechanisms of securing urban equity were, by default, reduced to technocratic questions of lower academic value than contributions to the big urban debates of the day. Simultaneously, in the arenas of urban politics, the stress on civil society overshadowed the action to push political parties to prioritise reform in cities, the potentially progressive impact of the core urban professions and the structuring power of local state bureaucracy. Possibly inadvertently, the question of how practically cities could contribute to making a fairer world dropped down the urban agenda.

Progressive forces may have inadvertently contributed to the dilution of once dominant forms of state-centred provision of urban welfare, but it is now clear that the long-held Northern assumption of a commitment to minimum urban services standards, the existence of a reliable social safety net for the urban poor or an inclusive planning code that operated equitably across all quarters of the city is under threat. Worse, there is not much imagination about how to rectify the situation (Mayer, 2013). Across the western world, the certainty of governments being able to uphold fair city management is currently in crisis. Decades of neoliberal state retreat and, more recently, austerity and fiscal crisis have left the urban poor exposed and unprotected (Wacquant, 2001). Under these conditions any expectations from urban residents of state action to uphold fairness are eroded. Even in rich societies, the urban future is bleaker than before, especially for the urban poor. The vision of a fair city needs reconstruction.

In the global South the situation is different. Early twentieth-century urban planning and public investment in the built environment typically served only the interests of the foreign and local elite, largely ignoring the conditions of the most vulnerable of the city. That changed in limited ways with the rise of global development finance and donor support that saw the introduction of sector-specific programmes aimed at providing for basic needs such as access to water and sanitation or low income housing (Simon, 1992; Gilbert and Gugler, 1994). Only later in the century was there an endogenous focus on urban social protection, and then this was triggered by debates on what the urban poor themselves could do to improve their livelihoods in cities when faced with unemployment and other forms of exclusion (Moser, 1998).

More recently, across the global South the (uneven) provision of city-scale social safety policies based on values of justice, equity or fairness are ascendant. There is also a revived interest in the collective benefits that might be derived from investments in urban planning (UN-HABITAT, 2009). Leading the way in the drive to secure the public good of cities is the relatively simple expansion of individual and household social protection (Ballard, 2013). Boosted by economic growth and the demands of an expanding middle class, there is also rising evidence of investment in the built environment beyond the individual home, through mass subsidies on public transport (Levinson et al, 2002). Even while extensive private (often securitised) development for the elite is occurring in the rapidly expanding cities of emerging markets (Lemanski, 2006; Douglass and Huang, 2007), the issue of how to plan and manage the whole city fairly is a concern that is openly debated in a growing number of places – Medellín providing one well-recognised example (Dávila, 2013). Entrenching universal protection in emerging market cities and ensuring equal access to jobs, services, housing and quality of life though public access to fresh air and water, safety and so on is, however, a relatively new area of public policy and, despite innovations, there is a long way to go in securing even minimal rights for the majority of urban residents. Many cities and towns continue to lack even the most basic minimum household service levels, crippling opportunities for the urban poor (Mitlin and Satterthwaite, 2013).

The current drive for greater fairness is perhaps most active in the untenably unequal cities of middle-income countries, where the Gini co-efficient of inequality is often over 50. Here there is (in theory) enough money to effect redistribution, but the lack of institutional capacity and political will means universal welfare support is not achieved. For the majority of cities in low-income nations, where comprehensive welfare and universal planning protection through subsidies, by-laws or planning codes, are usually absent, fairness is an even more distant ideal. In low-income contexts where local states are weak, a discussion about fairness typically only gets onto the political agenda through efforts at urban poverty reduction and building community capacities, such as fostering savings schemes, to negotiate limited resources for the excluded (see Wratten, 1995; UN-HABITAT, 2009; Satterthwaite and Mitlin, 2013 for overviews).

Given the global diversity of city experiences and institutional capabilities, there can be no readily held common scholarly understanding of what fairness in a city might mean or how fairness might be achieved. Superficial congruence of Northern and Southern urban realities, brought about by the retreat of the state in the North and the rise of some protection in the South, suggests that there may be more common ground than ever before in looking for utopian ideas that have global traction. There is as yet no universal 'Fair city' imaginary, though it is possible that the targets and indicators of the SDG process will inadvertently define this baseline, just as the forthcoming debates in HABITAT III to the 'right to the city' may create a global urban standard (UN, 2015).

It is worth starting with ideas that already exist. A rich body of material and practice informs an interrogation of the values and mechanisms that the fair city ideal might encompass in and across different contexts. Looking backwards in this way is sensible as it is unlikely that aspirations for a fair city future will ignore the long tradition of utopian thinking about cities and early indications are that old ideas are being incorporated into an emerging discourse on the future city (compare UN-HABITAT, 2013). Mindful of the imperative of contemporary relevance and the growing disparity in urban realities that any utopian notion must address, it is, however, useful to reflect on the ideological antecedents of fair urban development as present day informants to new proposals. Of special concern is the way these utopian ideas articulate with changing practices of urban management, especially in contexts where the governance and administrative regimes differ from those in Western Europe where many of the practices of city-scale redistribution were forged.

Twentieth-century utopian thinking on the city

Early twentieth-century utopian ideals had and continue to have real impact on the form that many cities have taken. In other words, how leaders thought/think about cities has a material impact in the construction of the built environment, modes of management, human expectations of ecosystems and the social and economic relationships of citizens. There is currently something of a renaissance in utopian writings, especially around notions of the good city and the right to the city (Samara et al, 2012), and also around urban resilience (Pelling, 2011) but it is unclear which utopian discourses will influence and refresh the urban transitions of the twenty-first century in line with the post-2015 agenda, or how they will be translated into action.

Vast amounts have been written about the early twentieth-century utopian urban planners (Paddison et al, 2009). A good deal of this history of urbanism is dedicated to the work of the modernist trailblazers like Ebenezer Howard, Frank Lloyd Wright and Le Corbusier. Given how much has been written in critique of modernist planning, it is useful to remember that their primary ambition was a progressive agenda concerned with the restructuring of power through the reconfiguration of urban space. All of these men understood their task as an act of urban reconstruction to counter the prevailing decadence and inequality of the past (Hall, 1996; Simon, Chapter Three, this volume). In his authoritative overview, the urban historian Fishman (1982) reminds us that each man recognised that his experimental prescriptions for urban form took place in a wider socio-political context and a consciousness that their utopian master plans would generally not be implemented on a blank slate. This kind of grounded utopianism is consistent with recent thinking of locally constructed or translational knowledge and practice (Parnell and Pieterse, 2015). It also ultimately underlies much subsequent evolution in planning theory and associated practice, to the extent that its heritage and ongoing relevance are clearly discernible in all three main chapters in this book.

Urban leaders faced with the particularities of local conditions might also find it useful to recall that the uptake of utopian thinking varied from place to place while holding on to a universal commitment to urban improvement and a growing acknowledgement of how fundamental human rights could be realised in the urban context. Howard's garden city was the most modest of these three models of utopian urbanism. He made a case for decentralisation and co-operative socialism that is not unlike the templates of some of the urban transition towns of today, with a focus primarily on the residential dimension and on household consumption (Howard, 1965). Wright (1963) was American and his utopian focus was much more institutional, looking at improving the potential of the state to plan settlement. Invoking the idea that ownership would provide a rational incentive for human action, he devised a model of deconcentrated (sprawled) urbanism that would facilitate a suburban home for every American family. By contrast, Le Corbusier (1987) thought that the urban ideal required far greater densification to allow for innovation, the concentration of the elite and the control of the urban population as a whole; a legacy being reinvented by Chinese and other large-scale high-rise private developers of elite housing in cities, especially those where crime is an issue. The imprint of these three idealists pervades cities almost everywhere and is etched into the urban planning codes of most nations, reinforcing the importance of fully understanding the intent and applications of ideas for how cities might be structured in ways that their protagonists thought would be fairer (Hall, 1996, see also Simon, Chapter Three, this volume).

What these ideas, although divergent, all assumed was the endorsement of a notion of fundamental human rights, effective local democracy, consensus on minimum service levels for the built environment and enforced standards for personal service consumption, a state with some capacity to redistribute resources (including at the local scale) and a comprehensive planning machinery that created the value base, procedural arrangements and enforcement capacity for managing a city in the collective interest. As the expansive literature on social polarisation and poverty in Europe, North America and Australasia attests, implementation of the utopian ideals fell far short of delivering a fair city even in places where the preconditions for their achievement were in place. In cities of the global South where cities are characterised by the absence of local democracy, the paucity of municipal capacity, gaps in data, fiscal deficits and a general lack of legitimacy for government, the utopian visions were either corrupted and applied to the elite or never made any impact at all.

For many commentators, the ideas of Howard, Wright and le Corbusier (that focus on urban form rather than urban consumption or quality of life) are now not only outdated but they fail to speak to the individual fears and aspirations of twenty-first century urban identity (Parnell et al, 2009; Roy, 2009; Myers, 2011). They also fail to engage effectively with the pervasive urban informality and illegality of the majority of cities and towns. The urban centre of gravity is now located predominantly in the global South, where most future urban population growth will also occur. These cities are rarely associated with notions of the public good, equity or fairness (unless the Chinese model is seen as an expression of the collective national good advanced through an inclusive, 'harmonious' urban developmental strategy) (Chen, 2014). Outside China it is the blatant unfairness of the extraordinarily high levels of inequality that cities of the South exhibit and their shocking service backlogs that are their leitmotiv. These urban places, characterised by dystopic images of collapsed states, ecological disaster and unchecked urban poverty, are an essential part of the reality which the global vision of a fair city must address (Davis, 2004).

In a controversial depiction of cities of the South, Davis (2004) invokes statistics from a range of places to present the dysfunctional reality of the state of the world's cities today in which urbanisation and industrialisation have become uncoupled. To be fair, nothing he describes does not exist, and in many cities conditions are far worse than his evocative if un-nuanced account of poverty in the cities of the global South suggests (Buckley and Kallergis, 2014). The most pressing point to emerge from Davis's account is that dystopia is not an imagined unfair urban future; it is the dominant form of urban life today. While the overly pessimistic accounts of the current realities and the projected futures of cities of the global South are widely rejected (Pieterse, 2008; UN-HABITAT, 2009), there is consensus that the urban challenge for making a better world lies in improving conditions in the emerging cities of Africa, Asia and Latin America (Gilbert, 2007).

The question is how these 'unruly' cities, which are devoid of fairness or transparency (Pieterse and Simone, 2013), should or could be better run to make them more safe, inclusive, sustainable and resilient. Residents, organised civil society and a global community are concerned that development goals may be left unmet because of the oversight of the plight of the urban poor (Revi and Rosenzweig, 2013). Motivated by a combination of factors, including the acknowledgement that the world population is now mostly urban (UN-HABITAT, 2006); that cities represent a major ecological challenge (Seto et al, 2012); that highly unequal and impoverished cities are a global terror and health risk (Graham, 2004); and that greater urban prosperity in the global South offers massive global market opportunity (Monitor, 2009), there is in the urban SDG and HABITAT III a new impetus to reimaging an urban world. The overarching aspiration is that the urban trajectory is to enable a fairer global future. With this in mind, we turn to explore some of the most important contemporary utopian writing on the city. Unsurprisingly, given the pattern of recent and predicted urban growth and the escalating power of the G77 in the UN system, much of the emerging utopian literature on cities has the realities of the global South in mind.

Twenty-first century utopian thinking on the city

Like the late twentieth-century utopian urban literature, which was centrally concerned with the structural causes of injustice of the urban condition, the recent conceptual work on improving current and future urban realities has the resident at the core. It is true that the growth of population and consumption has generated a dystopic literature about urban life that blames (urban) anthropogenic forces for climate change and ecosystem destruction and which calls for the more conscious contextualisation of human life in the natural system (Seto et al, 2012; Folke et al, 1997). Even where it embraces the city as a site of hope, fairness in this rendition is about ecological footprints, intergenerational equity and interspecies co-habitation as it is about levels of living indices and gini coefficients (Mitlin and Satterthwaite, 2013). In common with the people-centred urbanists, political ecologists typically do not reject cities as the way for the future, but are taken up with transforming how the city and the system of cities work through value-based urban management and innovative implementation (Marvin, 2013).

For many urbanists, including those who have environment rather than poverty as the organising basis for fairness, it is the proximity of urban encounters that creates at the neighbourhood scale the sociability on which justice, mutuality and care depend (Ernstson et al, 2010). It is the formative nature of the urban experience that shapes individual and public lives as well as attitudes to resource consumption. For Amin (2006), this civic politics is the counterweight to the alienation and fragmentation of the neoliberal order of the late twentieth century. Establishing utopia in an urban world is thus a matter of politics; a politics the endpoint of which includes universal access to the infrastructure that supports everyday urban life. It is not just a material politics, but one that presupposes a citizen's right to the city, where freedom from discrimination enables participation in city life and culture, even to the point of dissenting from the majority views.

Friedmann also endorses the practice of utopian thinking and deems it a worthy, even necessary, activity for urban theorists, if only because it alerts us to tendencies in the present that, if left unchallenged, will end in dystopia (Friedmann, 2000). For him utopian urban writing has two distinct elements – critique and constructivist thinking. The latter is the ideal around which political coalitions and systems must be constructed to change the trajectory of the city. Friedmann argues that the exercise of building an urban utopian imaginary begins by addressing such fundamental questions as whose needs the city should serve, whether it is the process of building a city or the outcome of the built form that is important, and by what values should the utopian city be assessed? His emphasis on process, not abstract values like a rights-based approach, leads him to identify (in what may be a very western model that presupposes particular types of democratic institutions that function at the sub-national scale) the local state, corporate capital and civil society as the key actors in building a good city and goes on to discuss universally applicable principles for assessing the performance of utopian governance regimes.

Whatever the context, constructing utopian ideals like fairness at the city scale takes place in a complex, contested interplay of structure, agency and institutions. In the European context, the way that unfairness in the city has been expressed most recently is through the exclusion of migrants, marginalised people and groups. The literature on social exclusion in the city, applied to both the global North and South, is extensive (for reviews see Beall, 2000; Hills, 2002). Of particular note here is the practical advance this utopian construction presents for urban managers. With a focus on forms of discrimination including sexuality, ethnicity and language, what the social exclusion perspective offers is a lens into the operational issues of access and distribution and not just the affordability of urban services. The notion of making the institutional machinery fair and removing even unintended discrimination and self-exclusion is thus a sophisticated advance on early welfare ideas that assumed neutral targeting, an unimpeded take-up of subsidies plus a basket of material, social and psychological support services for the poor. European cities gave by far the greatest attention to the utopian notion of social inclusion, although it is also true that this framework has been utilised to look at urban reconstruction and justice in places like South Africa (Beall et al, 2002) and the general terminology of inclusion or inclusive urban planning is now commonplace in urban debates.

Notwithstanding some attention to issues of inclusion/exclusion in the BRICS countries (Turok, 2014), in middle-income contexts the right to the city is now the dominant utopian discourse on fairer cities (Murray, 2012). The Brazilian model of the right to the city, which has been enshrined in the Constitution and law, provides the key point of reference (Saule Jr, 2005; Fernandes, 2006). Taking up from practice, the growing academic literature of case studies on how the right to the city advances a fair agenda includes contributions from cities like Cape Town (Miraftab, 2007; Parnell and Pieterse, 2010). As a utopian ideal, the right to the city advances the notion of fairness in four ways. First, it is premised on the legalisation of tenure on invaded or irregular land. Second, it articulates a vision of the whole city and not just individual or household strategies. Third, it accepts the formalisation of favelas or marginalised neighbourhoods into a unitary system of local governance, thus terminating the practice of competing and overlapping governmentalities within a single urban system. Finally, it extends the demand made in Habitat II for the recognition of the universal right to shelter. Based on a commitment to a universal claim, the right to the city embraces the political dimension of utopian struggle in ways that contrast with some of the earlier technocratic approaches.

Not all countries are attracted to or invoke the notions of the good city or the right to the city. In China an explicitly pro-urban growth agenda is promoted under the 'better city: better life' banner first deployed at the Shanghai Expo. It is underpinned by a philosophy of state-driven and controlled development of harmonious cities that is touted as the means to maximise human happiness and wellbeing (UN-HABITAT, 2010). Without access to the rich body of Chinese and other language texts, it is hard to assess what other alternative conceptions of fair cities might be prevalent outside of the Anglo traditions of writing on the city (Chen, 2014).

The SDGs and HABITAT III may provide a more specific articulation of what a fair city entails, but for now within the social development community, social exclusion and the right to the city hold the greatest general acceptance as conceptual and political frames for a fairer urban future.

Regardless of when they wrote, each of the theorists identified above adopted a means through which their utopian vision could be realised in practice. For Howard it was the idea of integrating green space into the urban form, for Wright it was the notion of freehold tenure and for Le Corbusier it was density and motorised movement around the city. For the social exclusionists it was the removal of prejudice in institutions, for the right to the city folk the imperative of the universal legalisation of informality. What is already evident is that even the most stylised ideas about fairness in the city rest on the assumption of a programme of change. While there are some commonalities across old and new utopian claims and approaches, there are also significant differences in the approaches, not least in the perceived role of the state relative to civil society (Parnell and Robinson, 2012).

Transforming cities can take a number of different routes, and, of course, some may be more effective than others, some better suited to conditions of affluence and some to contexts of extreme poverty. In shifting to the more practical literature on how cities have sought to transform themselves to become fairer, four general areas of intervention are highlighted: urban planning, welfare or social protection, participatory process and the actions of marginalised groups themselves. In some senses these are competing interventions, there are issues of which form of action, welfare or infrastructure, will provide the most cost effective and sustainable anti-poverty action. In other senses, these are mutually dependent means for realising 'the Fair city', where effective participation generates local knowledge and support for service roll-out or budgetary allocations. Juggling choices of how to affect a fairer deal for current and future urban residents presupposes in-depth understanding of the available policy choices. The following sub-section builds a preliminary understanding of the range of tools and instruments that are typically used in cities where fairness is an objective.

Instruments for promoting utopian ideals and building fair cities

Numerous factors, including the legacies of past injustices, influence individuals' or groups' ability to participate fairly in the city. These range from foundational factors ensuring wellbeing (food, water, money) to more complex factors like the freedom from crime and the opportunity to move about freely or enjoy environmental security. The first six Millennium Development Goals (MDGs) provided a fairly good indication of the minimum entitlements of residents, urban or otherwise; ironically, the city-oriented Goal 7 was less specific and much less useful in setting out exactly what the parameters of a fair development mean with respect to urban environmental services or neighbourhood quality, partly because the targets have been defined in very vague ways.

In the new SDGs, the debate over whether to focus on city-specific indicators for Goal 11 or generate other indicators that can be measured at the city scale is made more complicated by their being international goals, set to ensure at least a modicum of fairness regardless of where a person is born and lives, but the conditions and the data vary tremendously. Commensurability and comparability are not impossible. Similar types of targets can be defined through mechanisms including agreed minimum building standards, poverty lines and welfare entitlements that secure fundamental human rights (like access to water). While there are clearly major problems in establishing global benchmarks, beyond the SDG indicators there are no global norms from which fairness for urban inhabitants can be adjudicated. The high level agreements have their place but as places put different emphasis on what fairness means or how it can be realised in the urban context, it is difficult to track change without agreeing on some specific markers.

Drawing from the applied traditions of urban governance, the emphasis here is on the basics – probing what can realistically be done at the city scale, though as pointed out earlier, what happens globally and nationally is often at least as important in determining which urban residents gain, and which lose. Although there are clear differences in the underlying philosophies of the different forms of possible urban intervention in cities, they are not necessarily mutually exclusive strategies to promote inclusion, equity, justice or fairness. One example of this is the growing use of a commitment to green-city development that is overtly social in its agenda (see Simon, Chapter Three, this volume). Typically cities adopt multiple approaches to address unfairness.

Significantly, not all interventions to promote fair cities require large amounts of money. Clearly there are huge political and fiscal implications depending on how the approaches are weighted, and each strategic decision requires institutional capacity for action. In clustering activities into planning or built environment-based interventions, welfare or social protection interventions, participatory interventions and citizen-based action,[6] it becomes clear that all cities have choices on how best to foster fairness.

Urban planning

Cities are not naturally fair places. Land and labour markets concentrate wealth and privilege and the built and natural environments provide unequal advantages to current and future residents, as the built environment can easily lock in disadvantage, creating a spatial fixity of privilege and poverty (Massey and Denton, 1993). How cities are designed, managed and run mediates the extent and the form of inclusion and exclusion in them. This is nowhere more obvious than in the rapidly growing, typically under-resourced cities of Africa, Asia and Latin America, where cities with better planning capacity seem much more able to enter the global economy and prosper than those with weak planning, overlapping planning regimes or even competing planning systems. Competent planning capacity in a city in no way ensures that the needs of the public are addressed fairly, and it requires overt political will to ensure that the technocratic practice of planners serves the public good (Watson, 2009).

So who runs a city-planning machine? Or more pertinently, who will drive a fair city agenda though reformed planning practice? The traditional response is local government, though many cities (including in large countries like Kenya and India) lack legitimate democracy or functioning administration at this level. Given that planning is typically embedded in (local) government, this institutional lacuna is a substantive barrier to promoting fairness at the city scale. It is virtually impossible to achieve effective and inclusive practices of urban management that cover the social, economic and environmental dimensions of exclusion without a competent municipal system and a local political elite that is dedicated to promoting the interests of the excluded above those of the vested interests that often dominate city politics (Parnell, 2004). Even with clear commitments to equity from local leaders it is not always possible or even desirable to expand the burden on already overstretched and underfunded local governments (Batley and Larbi, 2004). In the global North, concern to expand citizen engagement beyond simple local electoral democracy has spawned a major effort to extend the interface between government and other parties, but this expanded governance process assumes the ongoing and effective operation of the state (at all scales) in the regulation and enforcement of the rule of law.

Fortunately for promoting a fair city agenda in the thousands of cities without competent local government or planning systems, there are other critical actors able to drive a fair city agenda and ensure the rights of urban citizens. In the case of the US and in the global South, where municipalism is not as powerful a tradition as it is in Europe or Australasia, it is often national government, and the powerful organised civil society groups and companies that stand in place for absent local states (to provide essential services such as water), that are the important urban players in advocating for balancing of the growth and redistribution agendas. Often states and civil society do try to work together. While most often the resultant city development agenda is subsumed under a competitive growth agenda, there are several examples of cities which, though working in partnership with different stakeholders and in consultation with global agendas such as those promoted by the UN, consciously hope to promote fairness (Pieterse, 2008).

As important to achieving a fair city as having competent administrators and professionals across government, communities and the private sector, is their ability to work together. In this regard, the notion of co-operative governance is as important as good government or effective inter-governmental collaboration. For many cities the problem is that it is not clear who the important institutional players are – either because privatisation or outsourcing has masked their role or because the roles played by traditional authorities or civil society in allocating or distributing resources have not been acknowledged and brought in line with the formal mechanisms of city management (Beall et al, 2014).

Regardless of whether it is a government, company or faith-based group that 'runs' the city inclusion agenda, how urban centres develop and are managed has enormous implications for the growth path, the developmental success of individual nations and for progress against world development targets (Kabeer, 2010). There is no single way to ensure that fairness is (or is seen to be) practised in a city. A few countries, like Singapore, have made great progress through strengthening planning and rigidly managing the urban growth process on the back of strong and uniform enforcement (Seik, 1996). Other cities, like Porto Alegre and Curitiba, in their drive to make citizens feel that the city is run fairly, have emphasised participatory planning around city decision-making processes such as the municipal budget. These diverse examples reveal that city-wide action aimed at including everyone through activities that are transparent and predictable confers faith in the fairness of a process. Historically, in western cities, the role of assessing competing needs, adjudicating the collective good and advising on the decision of greatest value fell to the planning profession, but this is rarely the case now as planners, environmental practitioners, professional engineers, health workers and many others take responsibility for some aspect of how the city is organised. In this fragmentation of governance the issue of fairness or the public good, the traditional preserve of the planner, has also been diluted.

Although there has been something of a renaissance in the view that urban planning matters for making the city accessible to the urban poor (UN-HABITAT, 2009), philosophies about how and why planners should intervene in the development of cities and towns differ and so practices vary tremendously (Watson, 2009; Porter et al, 2011). The general South East Asian experience, which has strong land use controls, shows that the simple concentration of activity in urban areas leads to improved prospects for economic growth, more cost-effective delivery of public service and greater scope to deal with particular environmental challenges. This is in stark contrast to the South African model, where, despite an interventionist national and local state, planners have almost not focused on urban land at all. Instead, cities have put considerable effort into promoting social inclusion through state assistance in housing and subsided service costs, rather than regulating the notoriously sprawling urban form though tightening land development criteria (www.urbanlandmark.org.za). But here too there has been some success in reducing exclusion: levels of both urban poverty and inequality have declined over the last 15 years on the back of a mixture of social grants and capital transfers (Leibbrant et al, 2010). What these contrasting examples of planning approaches suggest is that there is no blueprint for urban planners' engagement with the fair city agenda – but that concerted action by governments with resources can make a significant difference.

Effective urban development and planning exercises must be highly context-sensitive. There cannot be one-size-fits-all policies. Disengaged, top-down planning approaches of the past have been shown not to work in numerous contexts (compare Ferguson, 2008). However, there are four generic planning interventions that are widely perceived as providing a platform from which to promote inclusion and fairness (UN-HABITAT, 2009). These include:

Basic services and infrastructure

Denser living generally makes it easier and cheaper per capita to improve access to basic needs such as shelter, water and sanitation and to social amenities such as healthcare and sanitation, which is fundamental for ensuring universal access (Waters, Chapter Two, this volume). However, the tendency is for large cities to define their infrastructural priorities in terms of what they perceive they need to achieve economic growth and become 'world class' and competitive (compare Murray, 2011). Thus spending often goes towards 'connectivity infrastructures' – including telecommunications and logistical hubs such as ports, freeways and airports – for new economic sectors at the expense of public infrastructures that would benefit the majority of urban citizens and basic needs infrastructure for the urban poor. Alternatively politicians favour vote-attracting investments such as housing, leaving aside investment in public spaces of poor neighbourhoods. Building fair cities necessitates urban policies that integrate investment in big infrastructure, social spending and sector-specific interventions, such as housing, as part of an holistic agenda that enables access to the entire city (UN-HABITAT, 2010).

Public transport

Prioritising the needs of the whole urban population through investments in transport services and infrastructure, such as roads, footpaths, bus lanes and mass transit systems is essential to enable fair economic participation. Failures in urban transport policy effectively leave the poor stranded since they cannot afford long commutes and often live in badly located areas or on the periphery (Kessides, 2005). Massive advances in public transport that have increased the access to the city have occurred over the last decades, with many councils in poorer and fast-growing cities adopting the bus rapid transit approach pioneered in Curitiba and Bogotá. For the poorest of the poor, however, prioritising motorised over non-motorised transportation is unfair, as low incomes exclude them from benefiting from even subsidised public transport (Dávila, 2013).

Urban land and housing

The way housing and land markets function determines to a large degree the capacity of households to choose where to live, and therefore their ability to build up savings and make an urban commitment (Polèse and Stren, 2000). Policies in this field will have an impact on the maintenance of a viable community life, on the integration of immigrant groups into city life, and on the development of a viable approach for urban sustainability.

The insecurity of access to land contributes to the vicious cycle of poverty and exclusion. When property rights are absent or ill-defined – such as for people living on the urban fringe, in backyards or informal settlements – they will inhabit only makeshift housing (especially since they face possible eviction). Insecurity of tenure also means that municipalities are often unable to collect local revenues, and they are thus unable to provide essential services. Services are often procured through informal means, often making them more expensive (Gandy, 2005; UN-HABITAT, 2006).

A good public housing programme may operate towards mitigating tendencies towards social polarisation and economic decline. Slum dwellers can be granted a minimum package of rights, which could progressively evolve into a higher order of rights; in other words, there should be a formalisation process that evolves from de facto to de jure tenure (UN-HABITAT, 2006, 94; Satterthwaite and Mitlin, 2013).

The resurgent awareness that urban planning is a powerful tool for shaping the patterns of social, economic and environmental exclusion for many generations (UN-HABITAT, 2009; Watson, 2009) is most welcome. Efforts to address the major gaps that exist in planning capacity and practice, especially in cities of the global South, should, however, not overshadow the need to give greater attention to the durability of non-planning-based interventions that can make cities much fairer places. In terms of overall impact on urban exclusion, the most important of these is the large-scale social protection programmes that are typically funded by national governments.

Social protection at the urban scale

In the global North the package of welfare support varies hugely from city to city, but typically includes unemployment benefits, housing support, pensions, child support, free or reduced-cost health and education and a range of other social services such as disability support, heating subvention or community programmes. Some of these transfers will be direct to individuals and households and some will be made to the local authority for spending in targeted areas. Administrative arrangements for such systems vary but typically local government plays a major role alongside alternative service providers from government and NGOs (Ballard, 2013). In some British cities, where unemployment levels remain relatively high and where average wages are low, large proportions of the population now survive on some form of state assistance, with concomitant negative impacts on health and well being (Marmot et al, 2010).

In the global South the discourse of social protection emerged in the context of globalisation and crisis: a belated recognition of the need for alternative institutional arrangements to protect the poverty-stricken and vulnerable against frequent livelihoods shocks (Cook and Kabeer, 2009). However, the conceptualisation of social protection has since moved beyond a narrow focus on risk management and safety nets to encompass a broad range of socio-economic policies including social security, healthcare, social insurance, child protection and so on. The rolling out of these forms of social protection in many countries around the world over the last decade reflects the realisation that the state needs to re-engage in the social arena, playing a more active role in shaping markets, redistributing gains from growth and ensuring adequate investments in the human capital and welfare of the poor (Ballard, 2013).

That many social inclusion programmes operate at an urban scale is generally ignored in comparative social protection debates, where the emphasis falls on large, nationally-funded programmes such as healthcare, pensions and education. Very few cities are able to generate sufficient revenue to fund their own social safety nets, though some, like Mexico City, do so through locally raised revenue (Ballard, 2013). Most cities are, nevertheless, involved to a greater or lesser extent in the roll-out of social protection, such as housing assistance or site and service schemes, and how well this is done has a direct impact on exclusion rates and patterns. Social protection measures do not just work to alleviate poverty and reduce income disparities; they also enhance human capital and productivity and make some cities much fairer places than others (Devereux, 2009, 14).

Even in low-income regions, there has been a realisation that social protection measures are well worth their price (although donor funding often supplements local state revenue to pay for the projects). In cities in Latin America and East and South East Asia there has been a large expansion of social assistance programmes, particularly marked by large-scale cash transfer schemes, both conditional and unconditional, and social insurance and tax-funded provisions. Furthermore, in African cities there has been an expansion of programmes of regular and predictable transfers, mainly cash and largely unconditional (including social pensions and safety nets), with some significant successes. The Luanda Urban Poverty Programme is a widely regarded large-scale scheme operating in a city where, although there is plenty of money, there is very little state capacity for social inclusion (Earle, 2010). In cities of the global South, social protection measures have to support the informal sector, where most of the urban poor work in low paid and insecure jobs. To facilitate the shift into the formal sector, local authorities can adjust their regulations and laws to lower the costs and increase the benefits for people to formalise their businesses (Skinner, 2000). Other inclusionary measures that have recently been introduced under the rubric of climate protection and sustainability include large retrofitting of insulation, solar heating and other green innovations (Simon, 2013; Chapter Three, this volume; Silver, 2014).

Participatory systems and civil society action

Over recent decades there have been two parallel efforts to increase state accountability, both contested for their effectiveness in actually delivering greater power to poor urban households. The first is the decentralisation of government or the bringing of service delivery into the local realm. The second is participatory planning, an approach that has become increasingly common worldwide and is now often institutionalised in legal and fiscal frameworks. The shift in the scale and mode of governing cities is seen as an inclusive practice that is mandated by powerful international organisations such as the World Bank and UNESCO. Decentralisation and participation policies have attracted a very diverse, even contradictory, set of supporters. While many see such measures as a way of empowering people and making government more progressive and accountable, free market economists tend to emphasise the benefits of reducing the power of the predatory or overextended state. In this sense, decentralisation has almost been used as a synonym for privatisation (Bardhan, 2002). In response, Pieterse (2002) argues that decentralisation should be more than just about creating a minimalist state; instead it requires an understanding of a developmental local state where government makes space for markets to structure the provision of various social and economic services in ways that promote inclusion.

In its progressive form, the logic behind decentralisation is not just about the weakening of the central authority; it is fundamentally about making local level governance more responsive to the felt needs of local residents. Civil society must have a real say in local government decision-making and prioritisation, otherwise it is likely that it will be ignored by elites in government and no effort will be made to facilitate the redistribution of urban resources. In order to make any impact, civil society institutions that represent and champion the diverse interests of the poor and marginalised need to be strong and organised and they need consciously to deepen their reflexivity and critical practice, since they, too, are susceptible to elite dominance (Beall, 2000). Additionally, they must be committed to radical democracy and prepared for vigorous democratic contestation since there is no such thing as a neat consensus-driven politics that will ensure redistributive outcomes (Pieterse, 2008).

Conclusion

There is a certain irony that while, over time, urbanisation has made societies in general fairer and more equal, cities themselves remain inevitably highly unequal and unfair places. There are several reasons why cities do not automatically create good, just or fair conditions for citizens and why there are enormous inequities between cities across countries, regions and, especially, globally. The unevenness of opportunity in cities arises from the way they function as complex repositories of economic, political, social and ecological forces. How fairness is experienced in any city is also influenced by the fact that the built environment is largely fixed, and this means that current interventions create a physical legacy for the future (see Waters, Chapter Two, this volume), just as past urban practices shape the spatial maps of urban (un)fairness today. Making cities fairer is thus not simply a product of short-term policy intervention, but is the substantive transformative agenda of the urban future.

The longer view of urban policy is one way that the physical, social and ecological dimensions of fairness have to be aligned. Not all cities are endowed with the same ecological resources, raising issues about how services like water, energy and even food are moved between cities based on differential consumption patterns (Simon, Chapter

Three, this volume). Obviously, a fair distribution of public goods and services in a city (or cities) cannot simply focus on current demands, but must also project into the needs of future generations.

It is impossible to understand urban inequality and poverty without reference to the economic forces that shape the built form and structure urban life. The flows of capital and labour that feed or starve cities are greatly influenced by global and national regulatory regimes such as trade agreements, interest rates and product standards. I have argued that a 'fair city' agenda is not just about redistribution and social welfare but also reflects how macro-economic forces, big ideas and consumption patterns manifest and can be mitigated in different urban contexts.

Cities are unfair because of uneven natural endowments, differentiated histories and the uneven global and national flows of capital that create jobs in some cities but not others. However, local dynamics also influence the outcomes of urban development, determining the life course of citizens. Ineffective city responses to shifting labour markets, skills shortages, the spatial mismatch between jobs, houses and transport and the infrastructure demands necessary to attract investment are among the reasons why not all urban residents will prosper. City-scale interventions to enhance fair access to jobs and other economic opportunities provide one of the most fundamental areas of innovation in building fairer future cities.

Cities are not fair places because urban gatekeepers determine who will benefit from growth, elites mobilise to protect their interests and minimise their contributions to the taxes on which social redistribution depends. Unfair cities may also be the product of discrimination, not just material and political inequality. Countering racial, gender, religious and linguistic prejudice, the marginalisation of the youth and migrants and the issue of urban alienation are not simply issues of resource allocation; yet these are among the most serious cleavages in urban society.

The social inclusion agenda of cities is poorly formed or under threat almost everywhere in the world. To achieve urban fairness requires action at numerous scales (global, national, regional and local) and from multiple actors (governments, residents and the private sector). Fairness implies a consensus that recognises the claims of others and gives weight to public over private interests. Achieving greater urban fairness presupposes a capacity to learn and to do things differently; this is not a new agenda and there is a rich legacy of urban utopian thinking, albeit largely European and North American, from which we can and should draw while thinking innovatively about a collective, more fair, urban future.

Notes

[1] MUF commissioned this chapter. A draft prepared by Susan Parnell and Lars Lilled, from Göteborgs Stad, was circulated for written responses from teams of academics and practitioners in Cape Town, Manchester, Kisumu and Gothenburg and then workshopped at a meeting in Cape Town in March 2012. Versions of the paper were subsequently presented by Parnell in Bangalore, Amsterdam and London in 2013 and revised following two MUF sponsored meetings on the urban SDG in London and Gothenburg. Although this chapter is clearly a collaborative effort, final responsibility for the views expressed rest with the author.

[2] Notwithstanding the global significance of agreements like those brokered at HABITAT I on the importance of participation or at HABITAT II on the right to housing.

[3] The legal framework governing cities in relation to land title, building codes, air pollution or water quality is often a national responsibility.

[4] A disclaimer: the chapter is not concerned with the production of inequality and injustice, only the response to it.

[5] Given the richness of the literature on comparative urban welfare regimes the focus in this chapter, especially in the section on instruments for building future cities, falls on the emerging and yet to be built cities that are concentrated in the global South and which will be the crucible of any ideal of a fair city.

[6] Each of these subjects has a huge literature and the material cited here is indicative of the extensive case-based source material available.

References

Amin, A. (2006) 'The good city', *Urban Studies*, 43(5–6): 1009–23.

Ballard, R. (2013) 'Geographies of development II: Cash transfers and the reinvention of development for the poor', *Progress in Human Geography*, 37(6): 811–21.

Bardhan, P. (2002) 'Decentralization of governance and development', *The Journal of Economic Perspectives*, 16(4): 185–205.

Batley, R. and Larbi, G. (2004) *The changing role of government*, London: Palgrave.

Beall, J. (2000) 'From the culture of poverty to inclusive cities: Re-framing urban policy and politics', *Journal of International Development*, 12(6): 843–56.

Beall, J., Crankshaw, O. and Parnell, S. (2002) *Uniting a divided city: Governance and social exclusion in Johannesburg*, London: Earthscan.

Brenner, N. (1999) 'Globalisation as reterritorialisation: The re-scaling of urban governance in the European Union', *Urban Studies*, 36(3): 431–51.

Brenner, N. (2013) 'Theses on urbanization', *Public Culture*, 25(1): 85–114.

Buckley, R. and Kallergis, A. (2014) 'Does African urban policy provide a platform for sustained economic growth?', in S. Parnell, S. Oldfield (eds) *The Routledge handbook on cities of the global South*, London: Routledge, pp 173–90.

Chen, X. (2014) 'Steering, speeding, scaling: China's model of urban growth and its implications for cities of the global south', in S. Parnell, S. Oldfield (eds) *The Routledge handbook on cities of the global South*, London: Routledge, pp 155–72.

Cook, S. and Kabeer, N. (2009) *Socio-economic security over the life course: A global review of social protection*, Prepared as the final report of a Social Protection Scoping Study funded by the Ford Foundation, Centre for Social Protection, Falmer: Institute of Development Studies, University of Sussex.

Dávila, J. (ed) (2013) *Urban mobility and poverty: Lessons from Medellín and Soacha, Colombia*, London and Bogotá: Development Planning Unit, University College London and Universidad Nacional de Colombia

Davis, M. (2004) 'Planet of slums', *New Left Review*, 26: 1–20.

Devereux, S. (2009) *Social safety nets for poverty alleviation in South Africa*, Falmer: Institute of Development Studies at the University of Sussex.

Douglass, M. and Huang, L. (2007) 'Globalizing the city in Southeast Asia: Utopia on the urban edge – the case of Phu My Hung, Saigon', *International Journal of Asia-Pacific Studies*, 3(2): 1–42.

Earle, L. (2010) *Luanda Urban Poverty Programme: Impact assessment synthesis report*, unpublished.

Ernstson, H., van der Leeuw, S.E., Redman, C.L., Meffert, D.J., Davis, G., Alfsen, C. and Elmqvist, T. (2010) 'Urban transitions: On urban resilience and human-dominated ecosystems', *AMBIO: A Journal of the Human Environment*, 39(8): 531–45.

Faludi, A. (2002) *Making the European spatial development perspective*, London: Routledge.

Ferguson, J. (2008) *Global shadows: Africa in the neoliberal world order*, Durham, NC: Duke University Press.

Fernandes, E. (2006) 'Principles, bases and challenges of the National Programme to Support Sustainable Urban Land Regularisation in Brazil', in M. Huchzermeyer, A. Karam (eds) *Informal settlements: A perpetual challenge?*, Cape Town: University of Cape Town Press.

Fishman, R. (1982) *Urban utopias in the twentieth century: Ebenezer Howard, Frank Lloyd Wright and le Corbusier*, Cambridge, MA: MIT Press.

Folke, C., Jansson, Å., Larsson, J. and Costanza, R. (1997) 'Ecosystem appropriation by cities', *AMBIO: A Journal of the Human Environment*, 26(3): 167–72.

Friedmann, J. (2000) 'The good city: In defence of utopian thinking', *International Journal Urban and Regional Research*, 24(2): 460–72.

Gandy, M. (2005) 'Learning from Lagos', *New Left Review*, 32: 37–53.

Gilbert, A. (2007) 'The return of the slum: Does language matter?', *International Journal of Urban and Regional Research*, 31(4): 697–71.

Gilbert, A. and Gugler, J. (1994) *Cities, poverty and development: Urbanization in the Third World*, Oxford: New York.

Graham, S. (2004) 'Postmortem city: Towards an urban geopolitics', *City*, 8(2): 165–96.

Hall, P. (1996) *Cities of tomorrow*, Updated edition, Oxford: Basil Blackwell.

Harvey, D. (2012) *Rebel cities: From the right to the city to the urban revolution*, London: Verso Books.

Healey, P. (2003) 'Collaborative planning in perspective', *Planning Theory*, 2(2): 101–23.

Healey, P. (2004) 'The treatment of space and place in the new strategic spatial planning in Europe', *International Journal of Urban and Regional Research*, 28(1): 45–67.

Hills, J. (2002) 'Does a focus on 'social exclusion' change the policy response?', in J. Hills, J. Le Grand, D. Piachuad (eds) *Understanding social exclusion*, Oxford: Oxford University Press, pp 226–43.

Howard, E. (1965) *Garden cities of tomorrow*, Cambridge, MA: MIT Press.

Kabeer, N. (2010) *Can the MDGs provide a pathway to social justice? The challenge of intersecting inequalities*, New York: United Nations Development Programme (UNDP).

Kessides, C. (2005) 'The urban transition in Sub-Saharan Africa: Implications for economic growth and poverty reduction', *World Bank Africa Region Working Paper Series 97*, Washington, DC: World Bank.

Le Corbusier (1987) *The city of tomorrow and its planning*, Mineola, NY: Dover Publications.

Leibbrandt, M., Woolard, I., Finn, A. and Argent, J. (2010) 'Trends in South African income distribution and poverty since the fall of apartheid', *OECD Social, Employment and Migration, Working Paper 101*, Paris: Organisation for Economic Co-operation and Development (OECD).

Lemanski, C. (2006) 'Spaces of exclusivity or connection? Linkages between a gated community and its poorer neighbour in a Cape Town master plan development', *Urban Studies*, 43(2): 397–420.

Levinson, H.S., Zimmerman, S., Clinger, J. and Rutherford, S.C. (2002) 'Bus rapid transit: An overview', *Journal of Public Transportation*, 5(2): 1–30.

Marmot, M., Allen, J. and Goldblatt, P. (2010) *Fair society, healthy lives: Strategic review of health inequalities in England post 2010*, London: Global Health Equity Group, University College London Research Department of Epidemiology and Public Health, www.ucl.ac.uk/gheg/marmotreview

Marvin, S. (2013) 'Green cities', *Mistra Urban Futures (MUF) Discussion document*, Gothenburg: Chalmers University of Technology.

Massey, D. and Denton, N. (1993) *American apartheid: Segregation and the making of the underclass*, Cambridge, MA: Harvard University Press.

Massey, D.B. (1984) *Spatial divisions of labour: Social structures and the geography of production*, London: Macmillan.

Mayer, M. (2013) 'First world urban activism: Beyond austerity urbanism and creative city politics', *City*, 17(1): 5–19.

Miraftab, F. (2007) 'Governing post-apartheid spatiality: Implementing city improvement districts in Cape Town', *Antipode*, 39(4): 602–26.

Mitlin, D. and Satterthwaite, D. (2013) *Urban poverty in the global South*, London: Routledge.

Monitor (2009) *Africa from the bottom up: Cities, economic growth and prosperity in Sub-Saharan Africa*, New York: Monitor.

Moser, C.O. (1998) 'The asset vulnerability framework: Reassessing urban poverty reduction strategies', *World Development*, 26(1): 1–19.

Murray, M.J. (2011) *City of extremes: The spatial politics of Johannesburg*, Durham, NC: Duke University Press.

Murray, M.J. (2012) 'Afterword: Re-engaging with transnational urbanism', in T. Samara, S. He, G. Chen (eds), *Locating right to the city in the global South*, London: Routledge, pp 285–305.

Myers, G. (2011) *African cities: Alternative visions of urban theory and practice*, London: Zed Books.

Paddison, R., McNeill, D., Ostendorf, W., Parnell, S. and Teisdell, S. (2009) *Key issues in the 21st century: Urban studies* (4 volumes), London: Sage.

Parnell, S. (2004) 'The urban poverty agenda in post-apartheid metropolitan government', *International Development Planning Review*, 26(4): 355–77.

Parnell, S. and Oldfield, S. (2014) *The Routledge handbook on cities of the global South*, London: Routledge.

Parnell, S. and Pieterse, E. (2010) 'The 'right to the city': Institutional imperatives of a development state', *International Journal of Urban and Regional Research*, 4(1): 146–62.

Parnell, S. and Pieterse, E. (2015) 'Translational global praxis: Rethinking methods and modes of African urban research', *International Journal of Urban and Regional Research*, DOI:10.1111/1468-2427.12278

Parnell, S., Pieterse, E. and Watson, V. (2009) 'Planning for cities in the global South: A research agenda for sustainable human settlements', *Progress in Planning*, 72(2): 233–41.

Parnell, S. and Robinson, J. (2012) '(Re)theorizing cities from the global South: Looking beyond neoliberalism', *Urban Geography*, 33(4): 593–617.

Pelling, M. (2011) *Adaptation to climate change: From resilience to transformation*, London and New York: Routledge.

Pieterse, E. (2002) 'From divided to integrated city?', *Urban Forum*, 13(1): 3–37.

Pieterse, E. (2008) *City futures: Confronting the crisis of urban development*, New York: Zed Books.

Pieterse, E. and Simone, A. (2013) *Rogue urbanism: Emergent African cities*, Johannesburg: Jacana Media and African Centre for Cities.

Polèse, M. and Stren, R.E. (2000) *The social sustainability of cities: Diversity and the management of change*, Toronto: University of Toronto Press.

Porter, L., Lombard, M., Huxley, M., Ingin, A. K., Islam, T., Briggs, J., Rukmana, D., Devlin, R. and Watson, V. (2011) 'Informality, the commons and the paradoxes for planning: Concepts and debates for informality and planning self-made cities. Ordinary informality?; The reordering of a Romany neighbourhood; The land formalisation process and the peri-urban zone of Dar es Salaam, Tanzania; Street vendors and planning in Indonesian cities; Informal urbanism in the USA: New challenges for theory and practice engaging with citizenship and urban struggle through an informality lens', *Planning Theory and Practice*, 12(1): 115–53.

Revi, A. and Rosenzweig, C. (2013) 'The urban opportunity: Enabling transformative and sustainable development', Background paper for the High-Level Panel of Eminent Persons on the Post-2015 Development Agenda, prepared by the Sustainable Development Solutions Network Thematic Group on Sustainable Cities, http://unsdsn.org/wp-content/uploads/2014/02/Final-052013-SDSN-TG09-The-Urban-Opportunity1.pdf

Roy, A. (2009) 'Why India cannot plan its cities: Informality, insurgence and the idiom of urbanization', *Planning Theory* 8(1): 76–87.

Samara, T., He, S. and Chen, G. (eds) (2012) *Locating right to the city in the global South*, London: Routledge.

Satterthwaite, D. and Mitlin, D. (2013) *Empowering squatter citizen: Local government, civil society and urban poverty reduction*, London: Routledge.

Saule Jr, N. (2005) 'The right to the city as a paradigm of democratic urban governance', *Polis*, Special Edition for World Social Forum, 38–43.

SDSN (Sustainable Development Solutions Network) (2013) *Why the world needs an Urban Development Goal*, Thematic Group on Sustainable Cities, Supported by UN-Habitat, UCLG (United Cities and Local Governments), Cities Alliance and ICLEI (Local Governments for Sustainability), https://sustainabledevelopment. un.org/content/documents/2569130918-SDSN-Why-the-World-Needs-an-Urban-SDG.pdf

Seik, F.T. (1996) 'Urban environmental policy – The use of regulatory and economic instruments in Singapore', *Habitat International*, 20(1): 5–22.

Seto, K.C., Güneralp, B. and Hutyra, L.R. (2012) 'Global forecasts of urban expansion to 2030 and direct impacts on biodiversity and carbon pools', *Proceedings of the National Academy of Sciences*, 109(40): 16083–8.

Silver, J. (2014) 'Incremental infrastructures: Material improvisation and social collaboration across post-colonial Accra', *Urban Geography*, 35(6): 788–804.

Simon, D. (1992) *Cities, capital and development: African cities in the world economy*, London: Belhaven Press.

Simon, D. (2013) 'Climate and environmental change and the potential for greening African cities', *Local Economy*, 28(2): 203–17.

Skinner, C. (2000) 'Getting institutions right?', *Urban Forum*, 11(10): 49–71.

Turok, I. (2014) 'South Africa's tortured urbanisation and the complications of reconstruction', in G. McGranahan, G. Martine (eds) *Urban growth in emerging economies: Lessons from the BRICS*, London and New York: Routledge, pp 143–90.

UN (2015) *Transforming our world, the 2030 agenda for sustainable development: Finalised text for adoption (1 August)*, New York: London, https://sustainabledevelopment.un.org/content/documents/7891TRANSFORMING%20OUR%20WORLD.pdf

UN-HABITAT (2006) *The state of the world's cities report 2006/2007. The Millennium Development Goals and urban sustainability: 30 years of shaping the Habitat Agenda*, London: Earthscan and UN-HABITAT.

UN-HABITAT (2009) *Global report on human settlements 2009: Planning sustainable cities*, London: Earthscan for UN-HABITAT.

UN-HABITAT (2010) *State of the world's cities 2010/2011: Bridging the urban divide*, London: Earthscan/James and James.

UN-HABITAT (2013) *State of the world's cities 2012/2013: Prosperity of cities*, New York: Routledge for and on behalf of the United Nations Human Settlements Pro-gramme (UN-Habitat), http://mirror.unhabitat.org/pmss/listItemDetails.aspx?publicationID=3387

Wacquant, L. (2001) 'The penalisation of poverty and the rise of neo-liberalism', *European Journal on Criminal Policy and Research*, 9(4): 401–12.

Watson, V. (2009) '"The planned city sweeps the poor away…": Urban planning and 21st century urbanisation', *Progress in Planning*, 72(3): 151–93.

Wratten, E. (1995) 'Conceptualizing urban poverty', *Environment and Urbanization*, 7(1): 11–38.

Wright, F.L. (1963) *The future of architecture*, New York: New American Library.

5
CONCLUSIONS, IMPLICATIONS AND PRACTICAL GUIDELINES

Henrietta Palmer and David Simon

Accessible, green and fair – what is their contribution to a sustainable urban future?

> Ultimately, to achieve holistic sustainable urbanism, the dimensions of accessible, green and fair cities all need to be considered alongside each other, contextualised, and also assessed for synergies and trade-offs. (James Waters, Chapter Two, this volume, p 48)

Sustainable development is an interlaced concept and translations tend to provide it with sets of interdependent definitions, as the now classic division into the three dimensions of social, economic and environmental sustainability. While these definitions intersect with and enrich each other and aim to construct a holistic vision, they also project a set of embedded conflicts. As such it is possible to trace a triangle of conflicts, each one as a tension of values; the tension between economic and social sustainability as a property conflict – a conflict between the private and the public; the conflict between economic and ecological sustainability as a resource conflict – the conflict between people and nature, or between the 'city' and the 'wilderness'; and the tension between social and ecological sustainability as a development conflict – as environmental concerns, for example, increasing inequity between the global North and South, when demands from the global North for environmental protection in the global South hinder economic growth and public investments (Campbell, 1996).

These tensions reveal struggles of values and power and drag sustainable development into differing political domains. Are these embedded conflicts an unavoidable and inherent problem of sustainable development, in the ambition to structure development along separately defined but holistically connected concepts? Does the holistic vision provide a practicable framework for organising actions, or does it, by contrast, open escape routes for nice labelling of toothless paper products and unholy alliances? This book investigates the triple characteristics of 'accessible', 'green' and 'fair', leaving out the economic as a separate part of the construction (where ecology could be read as green, and social as fair), although forming an important element of both accessible and green. Does this new complex provide us with just another set of power struggles or is it advancing the agency of sustainable development in the urban environment?

Before looking further into what appears in the realms of each one of the three concepts, we should consider how to understand such a combined and juxtaposed set of concepts. Is the idea of a holistic notion viable at all? Introducing his three ecologies of *ecosophy*, the French philosopher, Felix Guattari (2000), resists the holistic approach in describing the interconnectedness of the ecologies of mind, society and environment. Rather, he sketches rhizomatic structures of connectedness, a concept more famously developed in *A Thousand Plateaus* (Deleuze and Guattari, 1980) and emphasises the heterogeneity of the three;

Unlike Hegelian and Marxist dialectics, eco-logic no longer imposes a 'resolution' of opposites… This new ecosophical logic

– and we want to emphasize this point – resembles the manner in which an artist may be led to alter his work after the intrusion of some accidental detail, an event-incident that suddenly makes his initial project bifurcate, making it drift [*derivé*] far from its previous path, however uncertain it might once appear to be. (Guattari, 2000, 52)

This view recalls what Simon (Chapter Three, this volume, p 92) writes of how non-enforcement of inappropriate existing regulations 'can itself be an important means of de facto support, such as permitting urban and peri-urban cultivation on open public spaces'. Practising sustainable development as a conscious responsiveness to local habits, behaviours, cultures, praxes, traditions but also to spontaneous local incidents, conflicts and disagreements, would be to elaborate and evolve the definition of sustainable development as the 'initial project'. Having these new and irregular contours appear would ensure that the three dimensions of the concept are constantly tested and reworked, and also safeguard them in an act of resistance towards an ongoing hijacking of the sustainable development definition by unsustainable agendas. Could we insist that sustainable development should be locally immersed before describing it as a theoretical framework? Would this possibly be the utopian 'anti-utopic' characteristic of sustainable development, shaping the relationship of its different parts, as well as contributing an operational basis for engaging with possible relational tensions? All three authors of the main chapters in this book come back to the local context as crucial in understanding and possibly translating urban sustainability. Hence, a possible conclusion would be to underline locality as a fourth and vital dimension of sustainable development.

New conflicts?

Sustainability has won the battle of big ideas, Campbell tells us, but the gap between theory and practice needs to be overcome. Campbell's challenging advice, as opposed to Guattari's, is to work on the negotiation of conflicts and simultaneously to promote a substantive vision of what sustainable development could imply for the city (Campbell, 1996). Seeing the conflicts as drivers, he trusts that new common grounds will appear. Returning to our initial question, which are then the possible new conflicts that might appear in the constellation of accessible, green and fair, and how do they advance the theory and practice of sustainable development?

Waters' chapter on accessibility has its starting position in the well-situated and embraced concept of 'density'. However, he points out, the many trade-offs within density, as the conflict of community cohesion and densification, adds up to an argument for questioning density as a means towards sustainable urban development. 'Higher density, then,' states Waters (Chapter Two, this volume, p 29) 'is not always an entirely positive goal.' Hence a reformulation and repositioning of urban density in favour of urban accessibility opens up what Waters regards as the needed normative focus of urban sustainability. 'Accessible' is ultimately defined by Waters as a tool which needs to find its *modus operandi* in contributing to the 'fair' city. Waters (p 46) writes, 'accessibility is determined by individuals' assets and social networks and so accessible cities explicitly consider equity concerns and the marginalised'. Access is also a measurement of power and justice, in reading *how* it plays out in relation to different parts of the urban population. Access in its *fair dimension* is primarily addressed here as *spatial* access to mobility and public transport, as a proximity and distance from the urban citizen to certain essential urban resources, or as access to different kinds of *spatially distributed* needs – public space, greenery, affordable housing or community facilities, which 'allow[s] urban populations to form links between sectors of society, and individuals to access social networks and community groups'.

In its spatial translation, access becomes a measurable dimension to implement sustainable urban development as 'a good tool for good practice and planning but also as a means to promote societal wellbeing'. However, as Waters remarks, there are possible trade-offs between the dimensions of urban accessibility. A conflict of general accessibility and access to green space could be one, since new transport infrastructure (as the means to improve accessibility) is often developed on open urban land (if there is any), especially when passing less vocal or powerful neighbourhoods, thereby possibly impeding access to that land. As we have seen in the light of increased urban immigration and social stratification in Sweden, infrastructure for public transport can also become control functions for immigration services, police forces or any private company that has undertaken that particular societal mechanism, as a conflict over access and the inclusiveness of the fair city.[1]

We could imagine the accessible city to be incarnated even further, with dimensions beyond the spatial, not only as access to information is enhanced in the contemporary popular smart city concept, but also as access to *knowledge* and *experience*. This could possibly release accessibility from its immediate asymmetrical connotations of having less or more access to the city as being proportional to the presences of material public or private assets. If local knowledge and experience are validated in building the transition towards a zero CO_2 future, the accessible city should promote accessibility to different sources of knowledge. In a critique of the centrally controlled technology of the smart city, Saskia Sassen urges access to local knowledge:

> every neighborhood has knowledge about the city that is different from the knowledge of the center, of the city government, of its elites and experts. Small children know their neighborhood in a different way from adults, and not just because they are shorter and closer to the ground. The homeless person in New York City may know more, sadly, about the practices and habits of rats across the cycle of day and night, summer and winter, than the best urban expert. (Sassen, 2013, x)

Accessibility is a relational concept between the urban citizen and the city, and understood as access to knowledge it also encourages direct engagement and interaction by the citizens with their lived urban environment.

Also for the green city, fairness appears as an original guiding principle. The green city, as referred to by Simon, has its western origin in Ebenezer Howard's inclusive agenda for the garden city; a combination of the best of two worlds – the social mobilisation and cohesion of the city-dwellers in terms of associations and radical discussion groups, and the self-sufficiency of the countryside's agricultural practitioners. Beyond the green lushness of the vision, it also encompassed rental housing conditions in contrast to private property, and still today, radical ideas of transformation of the monetary system (Fishman, 1982). As Howard's garden city was a bricolage of contemporary ideas of the late nineteenth century, it did not include some of the challenges encountered by the green city of today. Climate change is, as Simon points out, the urgent challenge that directly gives new impetus for urban transformative approaches, positioning the green city in the foreground with its capacity for mitigation. However, as Naomi Klein effectively informs us, as a consequence of capitalism's enclosures and exploitations of resources, climate change cannot be managed or avoided without a social agenda, bringing justice and fairness to the centre of transformative action (Klein, 2014). Another 'new' stress on the global environment is the eradication of pollinating bees and other 'provisioning services' by nature, which has informed a green urban mind-set with the importance of ecosystem services. But even in this radical understanding of a balanced relationship between nature and humans, Simon shows how the monetisation and hence attributed monetary value of the services opens up the commoditisation and interchangeability of different ecosystem services. As an example, a grove of trees removed by a developer could be replaced by green roof tops in the new developments. Values such as the beauty, shade, micro-climate, identity and the historical connectedness of the grove, are substituted in a functional greening equation with 'invisible' carpets of sedum plants on the tops of high-rise buildings. Besides leading to 'distortions or perverse results' (Chapter Three, this volume, p 83), this shows the dilemma of *definition* – since we can name a thing, it can be quantified and commoditised. Qualitative values on the other hand, are imprecise and like the 'event-incident', split definition into a filigree of meanings. The uniqueness and strength of the 'green city' concept, in relation to 'accessible' and 'fair', is its immediate translation into aesthetic and qualitative values.

The above-mentioned conflicts are, however, still aligned with the previously defined *development conflict*, where ecological modernisation promotes elite utopian visions on the behalf of social development, the presence of which in a sustainability agenda 'presents itself as an oxymoron'. 'At one extreme' Simon (p 73) writes, 'the tensions are regarded as minimal and the likely changes therefore mainly cosmetic or incremental. At the other extreme, perspectives like ecological Marxism hold that the underlying contradictions within capitalist relations of production are so profound that resolution is impossible.' Even an apparently indisputable agenda such as the greening of brownfields has its contestations as it puts certain green interests before local access to jobs. However, in relation to the green and brown agendas, working on the conflict is, as Simon (p 69) puts it, 'achievable since they do have shared concerns with intergenerational equity and sustainable resource utilisation'. Here Simon directly proposes, in line with Campbell's suggestion, new common grounds for the conflicting concepts, advancing the agency of sustainable development.

If both the 'accessible' and the 'green' dimensions of our trichotomous definition need to be inscribed into 'fair' in order to give sustainable development a normative direction, what new conflicts, if any, are then to be found in the dimension of fair? As Parnell writes (Chapter Four, this volume, p 116), 'Given the global diversity of city experiences and institutional capabilities, there can be no readily held common scholarly understanding of what fairness in a city might mean or how fairness might be achieved.' Despite the long presence of the just city agenda, she claims that the challenge of making cities fairer has never been larger; whereas in the cities of the North neoliberalism has eroded the tradition of strong safety nets and public interest protection, and in the cities of the South, where planning and social-protection traditions and institutions are partly lacking, fast urbanisation and the impact of climate change is pushing the poor city dwellers further into unjust living conditions and pulling the rising middle class into gated enclaves.

Parnell brings forward *a perspective from the South* as a 'new' precondition for the fair city. In order to formulate a general understanding of the fair city, beyond what already is extensively elaborated on in the theory of the just city, she points out that it has to be applicable to the city of the global South and its imperatives, since making a better world requires improving the urban conditions in the emerging cities of Africa, Asia and Latin America. Reading contemporary urban utopias, Parnell concludes that just actions take place within the sociability on the neighbourhood scale, as counterweight to alienation and the fragmentation caused by the neoliberal order. A fair city, she continues, is then a matter of politics as an access to everyday life supportive infrastructures – not only in its material condition but also in enabling participation in the urban making, no matter what a person's gender, race, cast, class or cultural identity is. Here Parnell finds yet another contemporary contribution to the fair city, in the institutional reworking around discriminatory mechanisms of exclusion. Rather than exposing tensions between accessible, green and fair, Parnell confirms the reading of the other two concepts as a normative production of the fair city, where the fair city plays out in the intersection of welfare support, local management, institutional capacity, land control, public infrastructure, resources distribution as well as macro-economics flows and geographical conditions.

'Achieving greater urban fairness presupposes a capacity to learn and to do things differently', concludes Parnell (p 137). To work on the conflicts, to access new knowledge, to be sensitive to local context and locally made 'eruptions' will help us in advancing urban sustainable development. The notion of the four dimensions of our reality, as we know them as the three dimensions of space and the dimension of time, are not four different lenses and comparable understandings of reality, but four completely different ways of being in the world, unfolding into each other's presence. Reading 'accessibility' as a relational activity, 'green' as a qualitative physical presence, and 'fair' as the unconditional value of a better world, we can escape any effort to balance the three, and rather see them as mutually defined and constituted.

From accessible, green and fair to sustainable cities

This book has been organised around the three essential dimensions of sustainable cities, namely accessible, green and fair, with the main chapters examining their respective evolution, conceptual basis, current dimensions and key planning issues. Having drawn together the principal strands of each chapter in the previous section, we now address the challenge of integrating the three dimensions in order to advance a coherent approach to sustainable urbanism.

The first essential point is that there is no universal or unique way to undertake this integration, because each local and national context is distinctive, and the relative weight attached to each dimension will vary accordingly. In each situation, the status quo – in terms of the relative strength or weakness of each dimension on the ground and in existing urban and peri-urban planning laws and regulations – forms the baseline from which to plan and build towards a desired or required threshold of urban sustainability. Here we mean 'build' both literally in terms of actual construction and figuratively in the sense of revising or replacing existing laws and regulations to provide appropriate guidance and enforcement.

The second key point is that without an integrated and coherent understanding of sustainable urbanism as ideal and guide, there is little prospect of being able to make substantial progress in the face of the many obstacles and challenges. These take many forms, including technical, bureaucratic/institutional, legal, financial and political. Some of these can be formidable, especially when, as indicated in the preceding chapters, the necessary changes affect powerful vested interests in land, property rights, economic activity and/or political power. As a result, it is all too easy for well-intended and progressive change to be blocked, diverted or diluted so that only the more technical, cosmetic and incremental changes are implemented. In other words, the changes reflect only some version of weak sustainability, probably informed by discourses of ecological modernisation, that ultimately do not affect the underlying power relations. Under such circumstances, attention almost invariably focuses on the 'easier' incremental steps. Moreover, isolated interventions in one dimension, for example, by committed environmental officials or those concerned with transport usership and accessibility, may not advance, or may even conflict with required changes in the other two.

As discussed conceptually in the first section above, this underlines the importance of holding the three dimensions together within a holistic framework that integrates research, planning and implementation, despite the inevitable challenges. In order to fulfil its objectives, this book needs now to take the final step and offer practical guidance to researchers, planners and other officials as well as elected representatives and other decision makers on how to take forward such integrated urban sustainability agendas. Almost everyone in all contexts will accept the desirability of promoting greater fairness in access to resources and facilities, although there will be different views about the balance between equity and efficiency. Hence the notion of fair or just cities provides a clear rationale to hold the three dimensions of accessibility, greenness and fairness together. As Susan Parnell writes in Chapter Four (p 108), '[t]he universal concept of "a fair city" provides a translational bridge between what is said and what can actually be done.'

The first practical step is to mobilise support for the agenda locally among the key stakeholder groups and hence for changing existing obstacles embedded within legislation, planning regulations and building codes, as well as to provide more appropriate financial resourcing. Experience shows clearly that having a *champion* as active promoter within the key institutions and committees is essential (Leck and Roberts, 2015). Such people need to be identified and supported in order to work across sections or departments within their respective institutions in order to influence thinking in support of the agenda. Linked to this is the necessity of bringing different stakeholder groups and institutional representatives together. In some cases, an appropriate mechanism may already exist, for example, a metropolitan local authority's strategic planning consultative committee, but often a purpose-designed *transdisciplinary* grouping will be necessary. Indeed, this might require two parallel groupings, one comprising strategic political and executive leadership to build and maintain support, and the other at an operational level to oversee co-productive research and implementation.

The process of finding and expanding common ground and building trust – the most essential ingredient – can be complex, slow and unpredictable, especially in historically or structurally conflictual situations. However, there is no 'quick and dirty' or technical substitute. It is important not to try to implement findings and recommendations from elsewhere or from generic guidelines distilled from diverse experiences without local debate, research and modification to ensure local 'ground truthing' and appropriateness.

Experience with transdisciplinary co-production shows that local authorities and other implementing institutions rarely have adequate in-house research capacity. Use of commercial consultants to provide 'expert knowledge' has a very mixed history and quite a low level of successful uptake of recommendations. Hence, bringing academic researchers into the team (and thus having research institutions as partners) is important for enhancing capacity and bringing more critical conceptually and comparatively informed perspectives to the table. This is the essence of effective transdisciplinary research and practice through co-production. Hence the remit of the operational grouping should include both research and its translation into implementation. Even where implementation ultimately is the responsibility of one or two institutions, having such a committee's backing and the authority lent by the partnership and the research integrity on which it is based is often very helpful and empowering, not least in providing support in addressing unforeseen problems that frequently arise.

Establishing and developing such institutional relationships is challenging and inevitably requires flexibility and willingness to engage in vigorous debate and even contestation both within and among officials and elected representatives of participating institutions. Just as there is no such thing as a neat consensus-driven politics that will ensure redistributive outcomes (Pieterse, 2008; Parnell, Chapter Four, this volume) as required to drive transformative (strong) urban sustainability, considerable effort and time are required to overcome antagonisms among institutions and individuals and hammer out workable 'rules of engagement'. The precise process needs to be worked out in each case, ideally led by existing institutional champions if already identified, but some will only emerge during the process or be recruited later. Outcomes are uncertain, time-consuming and not risk-free. There is no short cut but the process is crucial to building the required trust, working relations and 'safe space' that the partnership should then provide for research, experimentation and innovation.

A related consideration is the importance of retaining the shared knowledge, experience and expertise within the partnership, in other words in the public domain as a form of collective intellectual property. These must not become privatised, something that concerns many in the public and non-governmental sectors when private firms become members of such a partnership. This should not become a reason to exclude appropriate private sector partners because it can be addressed effectively by making the requirement of retaining common intellectual property rights part of a formal partnership agreement or code of practice, the adherence to which becomes a formal requirement for membership.

Complementing these governance arrangements and processes is a set of issues around implementation or delivery of interventions and projects to promote holistic urban sustainability.

As indicated in all three main chapters, *provision of appropriate hard and soft infrastructure* that integrates different parts of urban areas, addresses absolute and relative deprivation and enables other sustainable activities is essential. Criteria for prioritisation in line with agreed principles and guidelines will be essential, taking into account that bigger is not always better and that some relatively small interventions that fill a particular gap or provide a missing link can have disproportionately large direct and indirect impacts (multiplier effects). This is possibly the most readily visible deliverable and hence a key means of gaining validation and support for the new way of working.

Similarly, *coherent and effective land delivery mechanisms* are essential (Waters, Chapter Two, this volume). In most contexts, this will need to be led by relevant state institutions at one or more levels. This is not simply about new greenfield land delivery but also about maximising brownfield redevelopment to avoid 'dead', socially alienating and dangerous spaces and as a key part of integrated urban development with consistent sustainability-oriented land-use guidelines and criteria. As indicated by Waters (Chapter Two, this volume) and Simon (Chapter Three, this volume), existing conventional *land use zoning regulations and standards* are rarely appropriate and revision within transdisciplinary partnerships and through public participatory processes will generally provide broader support and acceptability. The objective should be to replace restrictiveness and rigid single-use zoning with more flexible guidelines that encourage spatial integration and mixed land-use by non-conflicting and non-polluting activities. This is the most effective way to reduce distances between people's homes, workplaces and commercial and social facilities, which, in turn, will reduce total and average numbers of journeys, travel distance and travel time and hence encourage a shift from private motor vehicle ownership and use towards well integrated, efficient and affordable public transport, with associated environmental and social benefits.

Use of *social spending and fiscal incentives* by local and regional authorities can provide important stimuli to encourage behavioural change in various ways that promote sustainability. Potential measures – some already widely used for various purposes – include public transport fare structures to encourage use and mode switching from private vehicles, prioritising poor and marginalised social groups; differential property rates or equivalent local taxes to affect particular land-uses, types of development in different localities and even household locational choice; the encouragement of individual and corporate greening activities on their own land that are consistent with and thus contribute to overall green infrastructure, water recycling and conservation and other appropriate initiatives. Ensuring *consistency of such measures with the regulatory regime* is also essential to avoid disabling conflict and, as far as possible, also unforeseen perverse outcomes. For instance, if public transport fares are strongly weighted to encourage short and medium distance travel to reinforce other incentives designed to reduce long journeys and promote multifunctional land-use and greater local senses of community, one perverse outcome might be increased private vehicle use for longer journeys, thereby adding to local congestion.

Underlying many of these issues, as with greening measures discussed by Simon (Chapter Three, this volume), is the importance of finding a *locally appropriate balance between voluntarism and regulation*. This might even change over time at different stages of urban sustainability transitions. Regulations can be catalytic in accelerating social and behavioural change which, once achieved, can be relaxed. Active and ongoing engagement by local authorities with other stakeholders and civil society, such as through transdisciplinary partnerships and participatory mechanisms with local neighbourhood and community associations, voluntary groups, non-governmental organisations and, nowadays especially, social media are also essential. The value of traditional information leaflets or newsletters to disseminate information to urban residents is very limited in most contexts.

Sometimes, when achieving appropriate legislative or regulatory change is impracticable, at least in a relatively short time, *non-enforcement of existing inappropriate regulations can itself be an important means of de facto support*. A common example is not evicting but regularising tenure and providing basic infrastructure and assistance with upgrading for squatters who have built shanties on open public land which meets their needs, provided that it does not preclude essential planned development. This constitutes an effective form of co-produced social housing. Similarly, permitting cultivation of crops on open land and road verges in urban and peri-urban areas, even if technically prohibited, facilitates livelihoods and food security for mostly poor residents and contributes to urban greening and other co-benefits identified in Chapter Three. Exceptions do exist, as in the cases of dangerously contaminated land or where it causes serious disturbance or contributes to groundwater contamination.

Finally, a new global development from 2016, involving all cities and local authorities, has the potential to serve as an important stimulus to making appropriate sustainable urban development investments and innovations. This is the introduction of a specifically urban goal within the set of 17 Sustainable Development Goals (SDGs) – also known as Global Goals for Sustainable Development – by the United Nations to run from 2016 to 2030. Unlike their predecessors, the Millennium Development Goals (MDGs), the SDGs apply to all countries to reflect the globally indivisible nature of the sustainability challenge. The formulation of the SDGs has been long and complex, with unprecedented consultation and participation within and between countries. Goal 11, to make cities inclusive, safe, sustainable and resilient, comprises seven targets and three supplementary targets with a total of 17 indicators. There are also relevant indicators within several other Goals to ensure good connectivity. Throughout the process, debate has focused on finding a workable balance between the desire for comprehensiveness and holism, in order to capture diverse elements of sustainable development as discussed in Chapter Three, and practicability. The latter includes cost, effort and availability of the necessary skilled personnel and resources within the multitude of local authorities around the world (Simon et al, 2016).

For all local authorities, the annual reporting, in association with their respective national reporting agency, will prove challenging in that not all relevant data are currently collected or easily available. Details are still being worked out but there will be UN monitoring and evaluation, accompanied by targeted support and capacity building to assist the process. This therefore represents a unique opportunity to use the targets and indicators to stimulate political leaders and local authority officials to get to grips with the practicalities of promoting sustainable urban development as articulated earlier in this chapter and elsewhere in the book. Regulatory change and appropriate investments need to receive particular attention. There is a risk that the process will be used cynically in a performative way to give a far more positive impression of progress than is actually being achieved, but it will be more difficult to do so if transdisciplinary and co-productive partnerships as advocated here exist and there is active engagement and participation by urban civil society.

External sources of support and networking

Various external networks and sources of support for such innovative approaches exist both nationally and internationally. Within individual countries, regional and national governments, parastatals and research institutes could and should be engaged with as part of effective multi-level governance where statutory requirements exist or other forms of support are available. Inevitably, some such relationships will be difficult or even conflictual if transdisciplinary co-production is not understood or liked, the respective powers and responsibilities are unclear, or if political parties with antagonistic agendas control different institutions. There are also national associations of local governments, of mayors, city managers and planners (such as the TCPA and TPA in the UK, cited in Chapter Three), for instance, as well as city networks.

International associations and networks such as Local Governments for Sustainability (ICLEI) and United Cities and Local Governments (UCLG), the C40 network of leading cities and Smart Cities Council also provide diverse forms of advice, practical support as well as learning resources and opportunities of various kinds (see list of relevant websites and Internet resources). The same applies to the Human Settlements Programme of the London-based International Institute of Environment and Development (IIED) and various national green building councils and their codes of practice and construction standards, some of which have now become internationalised (see Simon, Chapter Three, this volume, and the list of website resources).

Within the United Nations system, the specialist human settlements and environmental agencies, UN-HABITAT and UNEP, produce regular reports and other resources which are available on their respective websites. They also have special programmes relevant to particular categories of cities – such as UN-HABITAT's Cities and Climate Change Initiative (CCCI) and the Sustainable Urban Development Network (SUD-NET).

Final reflections

A common reference point in the three principal chapters is the seminal influence in the late nineteenth and early twentieth centuries, and again intermittently thereafter, of utopian thinking underpinning urban planning. Hall (1996) also point out that, paradoxically, much of the early utopian impulse originated in anarchist thinking (see also Friedmann, 1987). It is easy to understand how someone faced with a blank sheet of paper or the contemporary equivalent in the form of an empty screen in a computer-aided design package setting out to design a harmonious new form of urban settlement would be drawn to, and be inspired by, utopian ideals that somehow designed out or avoided the fault lines evident in the existing urban fabric. Implementation is a different matter; reality has a habit of intruding with all its complexities and contradictions.

One of the abiding imaginaries shared by all utopian urban visions is that of a better, greener, more egalitarian and better integrated cityscape. The bold visions of coherent and sustainable urbanism articulated in this book share those attributes and more but is this utopian? Many would argue in the affirmative. Had we espoused such ideals but failed to provide any guide to implementation or been actively engaged in urban experiments to do just that we might agree. However, part of the allure of utopianism is the unattainability of its visions. The world cannot afford urban sustainability utopianism. The imperative of implementation is urgent everywhere, but especially in those parts of the global South where rates of urban growth and expansion are rapid and the cities of tomorrow, many already under construction today, are emulating the unsustainable urbanism in the North and in the new Southern models of unsustainability in the Gulf region and China, in particular. There is little evidence of new sustainable Southern imaginaries that hybridise indigenous cultural and architectural designs with the best of 'international' industrial design, materials and lifestyles (Parnell and Oldfield, 2014; Simon and Leck, 2014; Parnell, Chapter Four, this volume).

On the other hand, there have been numerous references throughout this book to the problems and limitations of incremental or reformist change towards urban sustainability. Individual measures may help but unless linked systematically to a series of other changes, they are unlikely to make any significant difference to the overall situation. Institutional or political inertia and funding constraints tend to mean that the least ambitious measures are implemented and existing vested interests and power relations are not challenged. As demonstrated in these pages, 'strong' or substantive urban sustainability is highly unlikely to emerge via that route and certainly not within the short time required. Hence, the necessity for more ambitious transformative change to take interventions to a structurally different level and which was initially formulated in relation to tackling climate change adaptation challenges, is now increasingly being applied more generally to urban sustainability (Pelling, 2011; Pelling et al, 2012; Revi et al, 2014; Simon, 2016).[2] Applying an integrated conception of sustainable cities and urban areas as being accessible, green and fair in the senses developed in this book constitutes a promising way forward. In the words of Susan Parnell (Chapter Four, this volume, p 123),

As a utopian ideal, the right to the city advances the notion of fairness in four ways. First, it is premised on the legalisation of tenure on invaded or irregular land. Second, it articulates a vision of the whole city and not just individual or household strategies. Third, it accepts the formalisation of favelas or marginalised neighbourhoods into a unitary system of local governance, thus terminating the practice of competing and overlapping governmentalities within a single urban system. Finally, it makes universal claims to the rights of urban residents thus countering the mid-1990s objections of the UN system in recognising the universal right to shelter. Based on a commitment to a universal claim, the right to the city embraces the political dimension of utopian struggle in ways that contrast with some of the earlier technocratic approaches.

That said, it is important to avoid any sense of fixety or finality about such conceptualisations and aspirations, so that they can evolve to remain locally relevant in space and time. As John Friedmann, the lifelong advocate of making cities better places and chronicler of utopian thinking in urban planning, concluded his critical essay on engaged planning praxis,

> my image of the city remains incomplete, and I think that is proper, because no one should have a final say about the good city. Utopian thinking is an ongoing, time-binding discourse intended to inform our striving. It is no more than that, but also nothing less. (Friedmann, 2000, p 471)

Notes

[1] Under the acronym REVA (Rättsäkert och effektivt verkställningsarbete) – a collaboration between the Swedish Police, the Swedish Prison and Probation Service and the Swedish Immigration Authority, 2009–14 – subway exits in Stockholm were used as control points in searches for paperless non-Swedish citizens. These actions were intensely criticised in Swedish media (see, for example, www.dagensarena.se/innehall/polisinsats-mot-papperslosa-i-eu/).

[2] In this there is an interesting echo of Friedmann's (2000, 466) conception of the committed form of political practice necessary to achieve 'the good city' as being transformative. For all these authors, the challenge therefore ultimately lies in generating sufficient political will to make transformations practicable.

References

Campbell, S. (1996) 'Green cities, growing cities, just cities? Urban planning and the contradiction of sustainable development', *Journal of the American Planning Association* 62(3): 296–312.

Deleuze, G. and Guattari, F. (1980) *A thousand plateaus: Capitalism and schizophrenia.* Minneapolis: University of Minnesota Press.

Fishman, R. (1982) *Urban Utopias in the twentieth century: Ebenezer Howard, Frank Lloyd Wright and Le Corbusier*, Cambridge, MA and London: MIT Press.

Friedmann, J. (1987) *Planning in the public domain: From knowledge to action*, Princeton, NJ: Princeton University Press.

Friedmann, J. (2000) 'The good city: In defense of utopian thinking', *International Journal of Urban and Regional Research* 24(2): 460–72

Guattari, F. (2000) *The three ecologies*, London and New Brunswick, NJ: Athlone Press.

Hall, P. (1996) *Cities of tomorrow*, updated edition, Oxford: Blackwell.

Klein, N. (2014) *This changes everything: Capitalism vs the climate*, London: Allen Lane.

Leck, H. and Roberts, D. (2015) 'What lies beneath: Understanding the invisible aspects of municipal climate change governance', *Current Opinion in Environmental Sustainability*, 13: 61–7.

Parnell, S. and Oldfield, S. (eds) (2014) *A Routledge handbook on cities of the global South*, Abingdon and New York: Routledge.

Pelling, M. (2011) *Adaptation to climate change: From resilience to transformation*, London and New York: Routledge.

Pelling, M., Manuel-Navarette, D. and Redclift, M. (2012) *Climate change and the crisis of capitalism: A chance to reclaim self, society and nature*, London and New York: Routledge.

Pieterse, E. (2008) *City futures: Confronting the crisis of urban development*, New York: Zed Books.

Revi, A., Satterthwaite, D., Aragon-Durand, F., Corfee-Morlot, J., Kiunsi, RBR., Pelling, M., Roberts, D., Solecki, W., Gajjar, S.P. and Sverdlik, A. (2014) 'Towards transformative adaptation in cities: the IPCC's Fifth Assessment', *Environment and Urbanization*, 26(1): 11–28.

Sassen, S. (2013) *Open sourcing the neighborhood*, www.forbes. com/sites/techonomy/2013/11/10/open-sourcing-the-neighborhood/#72c772952fed

Simon, D. (2016) 'The potential of the green economy in addressing urban environmental change', in K.C. Seto, W.D. Solecki, C.A. Griffith (eds) *Handbook on urbanization and global environmental change*, London and New York: Routledge, pp 455–69.

Simon, D. and Leck, H. (2014) 'Urban dynamics and the challenges of global environmental change in the South', in S. Parnell, S. Oldfield (eds) *A Routledge handbook on cities of the global South*, Abingdon and New York: Routledge, pp 613–27.

Simon, D., Arfvidsson, H., Anand, G., Bazaaz, A., Fenna, G., Foster, K., Jain, G., Hansson, S., Marix Evans, L., Moodley, N., Nyambuga, C., Oloko, M., Chandi Ombara, D., Patel, Z., Perry, B., Primo, N., Revi, A., van Niekerk, B., Wharton, A. and Wright, C. (2016) 'Developing and testing the Urban Sustainable Development Goal's targets and indicators: A five-city study', *Environment and Urbanization*, 28(1): 49–63.

Selected relevant internet resources

Individual organisations

Atelier de Grand Paris is a highly innovative initiative exploring and promoting sustainable and integrated urban futures for the metropolitan area of Greater Paris through diverse approaches including highly sophisticated online visualisation and simulation tools. Its participants include researchers and activists with diverse approaches, perspectives and aspirations, making this something of a potential model for participatory city futures visioning.

www.ateliergrandparis.fr

Building Research Establishment Environmental Assessment Methodology (BREEAM), is the world's oldest sustainability assessment methodology for buildings. It seeks to provide a holistic way to measure sustainability across nine categories of research-based variables. BREEAM is now used in over 70 countries worldwide, making it in effect an industry standard. Various of the now over 100 national green building councils apply this or their own equivalent certification schemes such as that of the Sweden Green Building Council. One good example from the global South is the **Green Star rating scheme** developed by the Green Building Council of South

Africa (GBCSA). These are, in turn, affiliated to the World Green Building Council (WGBC).

www.breeam.com
www.sgbc.se
www.gbcsa.org.za
www.worldgbc.org

C40 was established as a group of 40 megacities worldwide sharing ideas, experiences and building support for tackling climate change and related environmental problems. Its expanded network now comprises 83 mega- and large cities, divided into megacities, innovator cities and observer cities. Together they accommodate 12 per cent of the world's population and produce a quarter of global GDP. Good practice guides and other resources and news are featured on their website.

www.c40.org

CityForm Network is a large UK-based research project investigating the links between urban form and social, economic and environmental sustainability. This relates particularly to density issues addressed in Chapter 2.

www.city-form.org/uk/research_findings.html

Citiscope provides independent journalism and coverage of global debates on the future of cities as well as expert commentary and analysis.

http://citiscope.org

Habitat III, the UN process on human settlements and urbanisation that convenes every 20 years, took place in October 2016. In preparation for this ten expert policy units were appointed. Each prepared a summary document and these resources (along with others from regional and thematic meetings) are available at:

www.habitat3.org/the-new-urban-agenda/issue-papers

Habitat Francophonie is a membership association within French-speaking countries focusing on social aspects of shelter and urbanism. Its website contains member information but also activity reports and relevant policy briefs.

www.habitatfrancophonie.org

ICLEI (Local Governments for Sustainability) was established as the vehicle for promoting and co-ordinating Local Agenda 21, one of the outcomes of the 1992 World Conference on Environment and Development in Rio de Janeiro. Today it is one of the world's largest global membership organisations of local authorities and it assists them 'to make their cities and regions sustainable, low-carbon, resilient, ecomobile, biodiverse, resource-efficient and productive, healthy and happy, with a green economy and smart infrastructure'.

www.iclei.org

Initiative de la Francophonie pour des Villes Durables is a recently launched initiative among the association of French-speaking countries to promote sustainable cities. Initially, at least, it is focusing principally on energy efficiency and renewable sources. The website has helpful resources in French.

http://energies2050.org/nos-projets/initiative-villes-francophones-durables/

LSE Cities 'Access to the City' is a research project on transport, urban form and social exclusion in the developing world, with particular relevance to accessibility issues addressed in Chapter Two.

https://lsecities.net/objects/research-projects/access-to-the-city

Mistra Urban Futures (MUF) is a unique international urban sustainability research centre based in Gothenburg, Sweden. It works through transdisciplinary co-production of practical, locally derived and appropriate solutions to locally defined sustainability problems. Its distinctiveness lies in its network of local institutional partnerships (Local Interaction Platforms) in cities spanning the global North and

South, and its methodology. This was applied initially within individual platforms but now increasingly through systematic comparative research across platforms in order to distil principles and guidelines of good practice from the diverse local contexts in order to influence global agendas.

www.mistraurbanfutures.org

Next City is a nonprofit organisation with a mission to inspire social, economic and environmental change in cities through journalism and events around the world. The website provides coverage of activities for progress in metropolitan regions across the world.

https://nextcity.org

Right to the city (RTTC) is an American alliance of racial, economic and environmental justice organisations. RTTC was created in 2007 as a response to gentrification and a call to halt the displacement of low-income people, people of colour, marginalised LGBTQ communities, and youths of colour from their historic urban neighbourhoods. The website offers useful synthesis material on cities and links to further reading.

http://righttothecity.org

Smart Cities Council is an advisory and 'market accelerator' body comprising corporate partners in the hi-tech and financial sectors and which seeks to promote their business through the deployment of intelligent design and digital technologies to build smart and sustainable cities with high-quality employment and living.

http://smartcitiescouncil.com/

Town and Country Planning Association (TCPA) and garden cities movement. This is one of the UK's leading professional membership organisations for urban and regional planners. As explained in Chapter Three, it grew out of the Garden Cities Movement and espouses progressive approaches to people-focused, sustainable urban design and planning. Its website is a rich source of information and practical guidance on these subjects, including garden city principles.

www.tcpa.org.uk

Transition Street, is an initiative designed to promote neighbourhood cohesion (add social capital) and behavioural change by means of discussions and working together to reduce consumption of energy, water, food, packaging and transport use and hence costs. Initiated by the Transition Town Totnes in Devon, UK, the first pioneer Transition Town or more generally, Transition Initiative. It constitutes a local grassroots-type initiative underneath this umbrella:

www.transitionstreets.org.uk

www.transitionnetwork.org/tools/connecting/street-street-behaviour-change

https://en.wikipedia.org/wiki/Transition_town

United Cities and Local Governments (UCLG) seeks 'to be the united voice and world advocate of democratic local self-government, promoting its values, objectives and interests, through cooperation between local governments, and within the wider international community'. It is a century old and has its headquarters in Barcelona. Its website contains diverse information and resources, including both its own publications and a municipal e-library.

www.uclg.org

United Nations Environment Programme (UNEP) is the UN agency specialising in environmental issues and programmes. It was established following the landmark Stockholm Conference on the Environment in 1974 and is headquartered in Nairobi. Thematic foci include climate change, disasters and conflicts, ecosystem management, environmental governance, chemicals and waste and resource efficiency. Its website contains diverse reports, briefings, practical guides and videos.

www.unep.org

United Nations Human Settlements Programme (UN-HABITAT) is the specialist UN agency on shelter and urban areas, working to promote appropriate and sustainable urban development, focusing on the transitional economies and low- and middle-income countries. Headquartered in Nairobi, its website contains a wealth of reports and practical manuals on diverse topics ranging from aided self-help housing, the CCCI and SUD-NET to urban governance.
www.unhabitat.org

Urbanafrica.net is a website hosted by the African Urban Research Initiative (AURI). The initiative was initiated in 2013 to support existing and future Africa-based research centres to inform and enhance the policy actors and networks responsible for sustainable urban policy and management in different African contexts. The website offers useful synthesis material on cities and links to further reading.
www.urbanafrica.net

Urban Sustainable Development Goal (USDG): Goal 11 of the 17 SDGs, being implemented from 2016 by the UN is to 'make cities inclusive, safe, resilient and sustainable'. It comprises seven main and three supplementary targets and 15 indicators designed to capture some of the complexity of urbanism and urban development in a holistic manner. Annual reporting is intended to stimulate local, regional and national governments worldwide to make appropriate investments and regulatory changes. The SDGs apply to all countries.
www.un.org/sustainabledevelopment/cities/
www.urbansdg.org

Additional websites and resources

The websites listed here are specialist urban media websites that provide useful synthesis material on cities, in-depth journalism, expert commentary and analysis and links to further reading:

www.theguardian.com/cities

http://righttothecity.org

www.urbanafrica.net

https://nextcity.org

There is no substitute for reading original academic papers – if you find a useful author follow up on further work by using either scholar.google.com/ or www.researchgate.net. The latter site quite often has papers already uploaded.

It is a useful idea to sign up for the contents alert (for free) of urban journals where issues of urban justice are debated on a regular basis such as the *International Journal of Urban and Regional Research*, *Urban Studies*, *Urban Affairs Review*, *Environment and Planning*, *Regional Studies*, *Urban Forum* or *Cities*. The journal *Environment and Urbanisation* provides an unusually rich coverage of efforts to make cities in the South fairer, http://eau.sagepub.com

Index

Page numbers in **bold** refer to a plate, numbers in *italic* refer to a table or figure, 'n' refers to a footnote.

A

absenteeism 64
accessibility 19, 46, 74, 129, 147–8, 152
accessible cities 6–7, 29–48, 146–51
action, community 114, 125
action, individual 86, 93, 162
activism 79
activity, physical *85*
adaptation 8, 62, 74, 76, 82, 84
affordability 23, 25
affordable housing 26, 37, 42–3, 46, 65–6, 148, 150
Africa 21, 85, 127, 133, 172
African Urban Research Initiative (AURI) 172
agglomeration 7, 18, 19, 21–2, 24
agriculture, urban/peri-urban 71, 79, 85, 92, 158
air travel 41
amenities 22, 28, 130
Amin, A. 122
annual reporting 159, 172
Asia 7, 37, 127, 129, 133
Atelier de Grand Paris 167
austerity 111, 115
Australia 22, 64

B

Baltimore, Maryland 43
Bangkok 37
beggars **109**
Bengaluru (Bangalore), India 63, 64
Biggs, R. 84
Bina, O. 73
biodiversity 26, 71, 84, 85, *85*, 87, **88**
bio-region 90
Bogotá 131
Boulder, Colorado 90, 92
Bourneville, Birmingham 64
Bramley, G. 39–40
Brasilia, Brazil 64
Brazil 123, 129, 131
BREEAM construction standards 93, 167–8
BRICS (Brazil, Russia, India and China) 62, 73, 111, 123
British Columbia 25
Brockington, D. 73
brown agenda 67–72, 86
brownfield development 88–9, 151, 157
Brundtland Commission 72
building materials 22
bulk buying 86
Bunnell, T. 80–1
bus rapid transit systems 131

C

C40 78, 160, 168
Campbell, S. 147–8, 151
Canada **68**
Canberra, Australia 64
Cape Town 22, 65, 85, 123
capital, human 133
capital flows 136
capital transfers 129
capitalism xiv, 64, 112, 150, 151
car use/ownership 20, 25, 26, 36–7, 41, 86, 93, 157
carbon emissions 19, 20, 38, **88**, 149
Carmon, N. 42
cash transfer schemes 133
champions, urban 3, 78, 154, 156
Chandigarh, India 64
Chicago 41, 85
children 23, 149
China 17–18, 21, 37, 119, 120, 124, 161
Cities and Climate Change Initiative (CCCI) 160
Citiscope 168
citizens rights 108, 116, 122
city models 26–8
city regions 11, 90–1
city traders **109**
CityForm Network 168
citywide measures 79, 90
civil society 124, 128, 134–5, 159
climate change 7–8, 162
  and fair cities 121, 134
  and green cities 62, 74, 75–7, 82, **82**, 85, 91, 150
  mitigation versus adaptation 8, 62, 74, 82, 84
Climate Leadership Group 78
'climate proofing' 87
clothing, second-hand **109**
co-benefits 8, 62, 71, 84, 87, 90, 91, 93, 158
codes of practice 93, 160
cohesion, social 26, 64, 148, 150, 171
Colombia 41, 44, 47, 116

Commonwealth Local Government Forum 78
community, sense of 23
community groups 40, 148
community life 131
community sustainability 32–3
community-based adaptation (CBA) 76
compact cities 20, 21, 26, 27, 29
  see also density, urban
compact city index 16
compactness 18–19, 36
competitiveness 26, 27, 37, 45, 128, 130
Complex Networks Analysis (CNA) 33
congestion 20, 21, 26, 37, 158
connectedness 146–7
connectivity 17, 29, 31, 44, 45, 130, 159
conservation 67, 93–4, 157
construction materials 87
construction standards 92, 93, 126, 160
construction technologies 79, 80
constructivism 122
consumption xiv, 2, 118, 136
  of energy/resources 20, 70, 122, 135, 171
Copenhagen **109**
co-production 5, 55, 158, 159, 160, 169
corporations, transnational 79
corridors, green 71, 72, *85*
cost of living 22, 24
cost reduction 89
Couclelis, H. 31
creativity 28–9, 31
crime 23, 25, 26, 27, 119, 125
Curitiba, Brazil 129, 131
cycling 19, 26, 33, 66, 86, 93

D

Dakar, Senegal *36*
Davis, M. 120
De Montis, A. 33
Death, C. 73–4
decentralisation 84, 118, 134–5

INDEX

democracy 92, 119, 125, 127, 135
Dempsey, N. 20, 33
Densification Policy (Cape Town)
  22
density, urban 12–29, 88–9, 148
  and accessible cities 34–5, **39**, 42,
    45–6, 47
  and fair cities 119, 124
design standards 87
Detroit, US 84
development, high-density 7, 20–1
development plans 27, 113
disaster risk reduction (DRR) 7,
  75–7, 82
discrimination 41–2, 108, 123, 136,
  152, 170
displacement 31, 38, 42, 170
diversity 17
donor funding 78, 115, 133
double glazing 86
Dovey, K. 16
Durban, South Africa **82**
dwelling density 13, 16
dynamics, social 40, 136
dysfunctionality 120
dystopia 120–1, 122

E

eco-cities 8, 62, 77, 79, 80
economic benefits 7, 21–2, 37, 38,
  134
ecosophy 146–7
ecosystem services 7, 71, 74, 77, **82**,
  83–5, 150
ecosystem-based adaptation (EbA)
  76, 82
ecosystems 74–5, 76–7, 82–5, 93,
  117, 121–2
education 33, 42
efficiency, economic 22, 24–5,
  48n1
efficiency, urban 19–21, 25
elevators 23
elites 8
  and fair cities 114, 115, 116, 119,
    135, 136
  and green cities 67, **68**, 80
Elmqvist, T. 85

employment density 13, 16
employment opportunites 24
  and accessible cities 33, 34, 37,
    41, 45, 47
  and fair cities 114, 132, 134, 136
  and green cities 65, 71, 74, 78–9,
    85–6, 91, 151
endangered species 67, 93
Ensenada, Mexico **15**
environmental impact 7, 12, 19–21,
  38, 41
environmental issues 1–2, 66
  and accessible cities 32–3, 41
  and fair cities 121–2, 125
  and urban density 24–5, 26, 27,
    48n1
Europe/European Union 18, 42,
  112, 114, 117, 122–3
eviction 67, 131, 158
exclusion, social 41–2, 46, 123, 124,
  127, 129, 132, 152
experience 122, 149
exploitation 91

F

fair cities 48, 107–37, 146, 148,
  149, 151–2, 154
fairness 8, 75, 77, 89, 108, 126, 150,
  152, 154
fare structures 157
Fashola, Babatunde 3
filters, natural 84
Fishman, R. 118
food supply and security 71, 79, 84,
  85, 158
form, urban
  and accessible cities 34, 38, 40,
    45–7
  and fair cities 118, 119, 124, 129
  and urban density 20, 25, 27
'fortress conservation approach' 67
French-speaking countries 168,
  169
Friedmann, J. 122, 163

G

G77 121
Garden Cities Association 65
Garden Cities Trust 65
garden city movement 64–6, 81,
   118, 150, 170
   Garden Cities Movement 7, 170
gardens 65–6, **68**, *85*, 87
Gauteng, South Africa 90
GBCSA Green Star rating 93,
   167–8
gentrification 40, 42, 114, 170
Geographic Information Systems
   (GIS) 33
Germany 25, 64
Ghana **69**
Gini co-efficient 116
global North 62, 146, 161
   and fair cities 111, 113–15, 119,
   127, 132, 151
   and urban density 17, 28, 47
global South 146, 161
   and accessible cities 37–8, 41,
   42, 47
   and fair cities 110, 115–16,
   119–20, 128, 132–4, 151
   and green cities 67, 73–4
   and urban density **15**, 17, 28–9
globalisation 1, 132
goals, development 120
   see also Millennium
   Development Goals (MDGs);
   Sustainable Development Goals
   (SDGs)
good city 8, 110, 117, 123–4, 163
governance 18, 156, 160, 162, 171
   and accessible cities 33, 42, 45
   and fair cities 114, 117, 122–3,
   126, 127, 128–9, 132, 134, 135,
   162
   and green cities 77, 84, 90
government, local 18, 35, 77, 91,
   93, 127, 132, 135
government, national 78, 128, 133
government, regional 78, 91
grants, social 129
green agenda 67–72

Green Building Councils 93, 160,
   167–8
green cities 48, 61–94, 126, 146,
   149–51
green economy 73–4
green space *85*, 124, 148
   and accessible cities 34, 43–4, 48
   and urban density 16, 20, 21,
   25, 26
Green Star rating scheme 93,
   167–8
green-blue agendas 7, 82
greenfield development 88, 151,
   157
greening, economic 73–4, 78
greening, urban 7, 61–2, 73–5,
   77–91, 157, 158
greenness 5, **68**, 81, 152, 154
greenwashing 72, 79
ground cover **82**, 84
growth, economic 37, 43, 73, 113,
   115–16, 129, 130, 136, 146
growth, green 73, 74
Guattari, Felix 146–7
Gulf region 161

H

habitat conservation 67
Habitat Francophonie 168–9
Habitat I 137n2
Habitat II 123, 137n2
Habitat III 2, 6, 113, 117, 121, 124,
   168
Hall, P. 161
Hampstead Garden Suburb, London
   65
Hansen, W. 30–1
harmonious cities 120, 124
Haussmann, Georges-Eugene 63,
   66
health 12, 19, 121
   and green cities 63, 65, 71, 81,
   84, 91
health and safety 44, 113, 137n3
health services 42
heat island effects 84
heating, district 87
Helsinki 23

high-rise development 20–1, 119
holistic approach 65, 82, 130, 145, 146, 154, 156, 162
Hong Kong **14**
housing 27, 39, 157
  and fair cities 114, 118, 123, 129, 130, 131–2
housing, affordable 26, 37, 42–3, 46, 65–6, 148, 150
housing, formal **14**
housing, informal **15**, 28–9, **82**, 131, 158, 162
housing, middle class **15**
housing, mixed 42, 65–6, 89
housing, right to 123, 137n2, 162
housing, social 42, 158
housing associations 42
Howard, Ebenezer 12, 64, 65, 66, 118, 124, 150
Human Development Index 2
human rights 118, 119, 123, 126, 162
Human Settlements Programme, IIED 160

I

ICT (information and communication techology) 31, 45, 47, 80, 130
imagination 112
immigration 43, 47, 131, 149, 163n1
implementation 91, 119, 121, 155–6, 161
incentives 18, 78, 86, 93, 113, 157
inclusion, social 123, 126, 127, 133
incrementalism 8, 62, 72, 73, 75, 93, 151, 153–4, 162
India 18, 63, 64, 127
industrialisation 12, 63, 81, **89**
inequality xiv, 3, 8, 23–4
  and accessible cities 38, 40–1
  and fair cities 108, 110, 111–12, 113, 115–16, 120–1, 126–7, 129, 135
  and green cities 67–72, 80–1, 83
inertia 92, 162
informality, urban 28, **30**, 119, 124

informal housing **15**, 28–9, **82**, 131, 158, 162
information dissemination 158
infrastructure 148–9, 156
  and accessible cities 34, 35–40, 48
  and fair cities 122, 124, 130–1, 136
  and green cities 66, 87, 88
  and urban density 18, 20, 21, 25, 26–7, 28
infrastructure, social 39–40, 48
infrastructure, transport 35–9, 130–1
infrastructure density 16
Initiative de la Francophonie pour des Villes Durables 169
innovation 22, 27, 45, 47, 79
insulation of buildings 79, 86, 134
insurance, social 133
integration, spatial 157
intensity 13, 17, 29
interaction, social 23, 25, 32, 44
Intergovernmental Panel on Climate Change (IPCC) 76
international agencies 78
International Institute of Environment and Development (IIED) 160
investment 18, 22, 81, 115–16, 130, 159
Israel 23
Istanbul 85

J

just cities 110, 151, 152, 154
  see also fair cities
justice, social 46, 148
  and fair cities 111–12, 114, 126
  and green cities 65, 67, 81, 150
  see also fairness
justice systems 34, 40–2

K

Kampala, Uganda **68**
Kenya 127
Klein, Naomi 150

knowledge, local 125, 149
Kuala Lumpur, Malaysia 46
Kumasi, Ghana **69**

L

Lagos, Nigeria 3, **30**, **71**
Laguna, J. 33
land ownership 162
land use 20, 72, 129, 131–2, 149,
  156–7
land use planning 35, 36, 47, 63
land value 65, 72
Latin America 127, 133
Le Corbusier 12, 64, 66, 118, 119,
  124
leadership xiv, 79, 108, 117, 154–6
Lee, J. 16
leisure 22, 67, 71, 84, 93
Letchworth Garden City 64, 66
light bulbs 72, 86
liveability/living environments 23,
  27, 31
Local Agenda 21 169
local authorities 42, 90, 92, 154,
  155, 157, 159
Local Authorities for Sustainability
  (ICLEI) 78
local government 18, 35, 77, 91, 93,
  127–8, 132, 135
Local Governments for
  Sustainability (ICLEA) 160, 169
locality 147, 157
London 42–3, 65, **109**
low-income countries/areas 40, 69,
  116, 133
LSE Cities 'Access to the City' 169
Luanda Urban Poverty Programme
  133
Luque, A. 79–80, 81
Lusaka, Northern Rhodesia (later
  Zambia) 64

M

Manhattan **14**, **87**, **88**
Maputo **109**
marginalisation 136

marginalised groups 28, 46, 83, 123,
  125, 135, 148, 157, 162
market opportunities 121
Marom, N. 42
Marxism, ecological 73, 151
Medellín, Colombia 44, 47, 116
megacities 168
Melbourne 85
'Metrocables' system 44
metropolitan open space systems
  (MOSS) 71
Mexico **15**, 133
middle classes xiv, **15**, 115–16
  and green cities 65, 66, 67, 69,
    80, 89
middle-income countries 1, 111,
  116, 123
Millennium Development Goals
  (MDGs) 2, 125, 159
minimum standards 81, 113
Mistra Urban Futures (MUF) 5–6,
  111, 169
mitigation versus adaptation 8, 62,
  74, 82, 84
mobility 19, 34–5, 125, 148, 157
modernisation, ecological 25, 48n1,
  75, 77, 78, 151, 153
modernism 79, 80, 91, 118
Modi, Narendra 79
Monzón, A. 37
Morris, J. M. 31
'multiplicitous assemblage' 16
Myers, G. 75

N

Nagendra, H. 63
Nanjing, China **89**
National Parks 67
nature, urban 62, 81, 83, 93–4, 146,
  150
needs, basic 2, 67, 114, 115, 130
neoliberalism
  and fair cities 111, 114, 115, 122,
    151, 152
  and green cities 73, 75, 79, 80
'New Americans Task Force' 43
New Garden City Movement 66
new towns 64, 66

see also garden city movement;
villages, model
New Urban Agenda xv, 2–3, 6
New York **14**, 42, 85, **87**
Next City 170
Nigeria 3, **30**, **71**
non-enforcement 92, 147, 158
non-governmental organisations
(NGOs) 83, 132, 156, 158
North America 111

O

OECD (Organization for
Economic Cooperation and
Development) 17, 73, 84–5
'optimal city size' 24
Oslo 65
outcomes, perverse 157–8
outdoor pursuits 63
overcrowding 16
ownership, community 65
ownership, land/property 118, 124,
162

P

Pafka, E. 16
Palmer, Henrietta 8, 145–63
Paris 63
Paris Agreement 2
parking 20, 72
parks 63, *85*, 93
Parnell, Susan 8, 107–37, 151–2,
154, 162
participation, citizen 41
payment for ecosystem service
(PES) 83
pedestrianisation **39**, 72
pedestrians 19, 26, 33, 66, 72, 86
Perdue, N. A. 16
peri-urban areas 158
permeable surfaces 92
'personal space measure' 16
Pieterse, E. 134
Pinelands, Cape Town 65
'planetary urbanisation' 48
planning, participatory 84, 114,
129, 134, 137n2, 157

planning, top-down 130
planning, urban 28, 154–6, 162,
170
and accessible cities 36, 38,
39–40, 41
and fair cities 114, 115, 118, 119,
125, 126–30, 132
and green cities 63–6, 82, 90,
91–2
plant species 92, 93
playing fields 63, 93
policy, national 74, 113, 137n3
policy, urban 18, 110, 111, 113, 135
political context 24–6
politics, urban 79, 92, 114, 122
pollution 37, **39**, **89**, 158
polycentric cities 26
Ponte, S. 73
population 7, 11, 12, 16, 119, 120
Port Sunlight, Wirral 64
Portland, Oregon 38
Porto Alegre 129
Potchefstroom, South Africa 40
poverty
and accessible cities 39–40, 47
and fair cities 116, 125, 126, 129,
131, 134
and green cities **69**, 80
precolonial cultures 62
preindustrial urban societies 62
prejudice 124
prioritisation 130–1, 135, 156
privatisation 114, 134
productivity 22, 64, 133
profitability 26, 64, 91
property rates 157
property rights 18, 91, 92, 131–2
prospects, life **109**
protection, social 8, 110–11, 114,
115–16, 125, 132–4
proximity 34–5, 36, 38, 44, 148
public good 8, 115, 120, 127, 129
public services 27, 33, 35, 47, 119
public spaces 27–8, 34, 43–4, 47,
48, 63, **69**, 130, 148
see also green space

public-private partnership 43,
   154–6
Putrajaya, Malaysia 46

Q

quality of life 2, 20, 26, 62, 113,
   116

R

railways 37
Randstad, Netherlands 38
recreational space 22, 24, 63, 71, 72,
   81, **88**, 93
recycling 72, 86, 157
redevelopment 86, 87, 88–9, 90,
   151, 157
redistribution 8, 113, 114, 116, 119,
   135, 136
regeneration, urban 88–9, 90
Reggiani, A. 33
regional authorities 90–1, 157
regulation 91–3, 147, 157–8, 159
   and fair cities 113, 134, 136,
   137n3
rental units 42, 150
residential density 12, **14–15**, 16
resilience, green 73, 77, 84
resilience, urban 117
resource distribution 32, 40, 112
resource efficiency 19, 26, 48n1
restructuring 90
Richardson, H.W. 24
right to the city 8, 110, 117, 122,
   123–4, 162
Right to the city (RTTC) 170
Rio de Janeiro **15**, 85, 169
road capacity 37
road density 16
Rode, P. 38
roof gardens 86, **87**, 150
runoff 71, 92

S

Saltaire, West Yorkshire 64
Santiago de Chile 24
Sassen, Saskia 149
scepticism, climate 76

sea level rise 76
securitisation 114
security, human 85, 91
segregation 24, 25, 41, 42–3
services, basic 130, 131, 135–6
services, key 24, 33
services, public 27, 33, 35, 47, 119
sewer systems 63, 93
Shanghai Expo 124
shantytowns **15**
shelter, right to 123, 137n2, 162
Simon, David 7, 8, 74, 147, 149–50,
   151, 157–8
Singapore **14**, **39**, 128–9
slums **15**, 28, 131–2
smart cities
   and accessible cities 34, 45, 149
   and green cities 62, 77, 79, 80
   and urban density 20, 27
Smart Cities Council 160, 170
smart grids 77, 80
smart mobility 34–5
sociability 122, 152
social equity 8, 67, 126
   and accessible cities 33, 34, 43,
      45, 46, 148
   and urban density 12, 23–5
social media 158
social networks 40
social protection 8, 110–11, 114,
   115–16, 125, 132–4
social sustainability *see* sustainability,
   social
socialism, co-operative 118
socio-ecological perspective 7, 81,
   84, 93–4
socio-economic approach 7, 78–9,
   93–4, 113
socio-spatial equity/justice 37, 69
socio-technical perspective 7, 27,
   77, 79, 93
'soft engineering' 77
solar panels 86, 93
South Africa 40, 168
   and fair cities 123, 129
   and green cities 65, 74, **82**, 86,
      90, 93
spatial scale 4, 5, 86–91

speed of travel 36
spending, social 130, 157
sprawl 17–18, 88, 119, 129
Stockholm 85, 163n1, 171
stratification, social 149
street lights 72
subsidisation 86, 93, 116, 123, 129, 131
subsistence 71
suburbanisation 25, 37, 89, 119
suburbs **15**, 64–5, 87
subway exits 163n1
sustainability, community 32–3
sustainability, ecological 146
sustainability, economic 145–6
sustainability, environmental 24, 25, 32, 73, 80, 145
sustainability, social 25, 31–3, 34, 46, 145, 146
sustainability, urban
    green cities 61, 62–3, 65, 72, 75, 90
    urban sustainability 2–4, 7–8, 131, 145–59
    weak and strong 4, 7, 61, 72, 75, 153
sustainability discourses 4, 46, 66, 72, 74
sustainable development 18, 46, 145, 146, 147, 148, 151, 152
    and fair cities 8, 107–37, 159
    and green cities 65, 67
Sustainable Development Goals (SDGs) 2, 107–8, 113, 117, 121, 124, 125, 159
    SDG11 35, 113, 125, 159, 172
Sustainable Urban Development Network (SUD-NET) 160
Sweden 149, 163n1, 167, 169
Swilling, M. 74
Sydney 26

T

Taiwan 25
Tanzania 42
taxation 89, 131, 133, 157
terrorism 121
Tokyo **14**

Toronto 26
Totnes, Devon 171
town and country planning *see* planning, urban
Town and Country Planning Association (TCPA) 65, 160, 170
trade, informal **30**
trade-offs 24–6, 29–30, 41, 47, 73, 148–9
traffic density 16
transdisciplinary groups 154–6, 157, 158, 159, 160
transformation, green 73, 74, 77
transition, urban 118
Transition Street 86–7, 171
transit-oriented development (TOD) 19–20, 35, 46
transport, public 19, 26, 33, 72, 86, 116, 130–1, 157
transport, urban
    and accessible cities 33, 35–40, 41, 42, 44, 46, 148
    and fair cities 116, 124, 130–1, 136
    and green cities 66, 72, 80, *85*, 86
transport hubs 41, 46
trees **69**, *85*, 150
trust 155

U

Uganda **68**
Ullevål, Oslo 65
UNESCO 134
United Cities and Local Governments (UCLG) 78, 160, 171
United Kingdom 168, 170
    and accessible cities **39**, 42–3
    and fair cities 113, 132
    and green cities 63, 64, 65, 66, 93
    and urban density 20, 21, 22, 25, 28
United Nations 128, 159, 160, 162
    see also Sustainable Development Goals (SDGs)
United Nations Environment Programme (UNEP) 74, 160, 171

United Nations Framework
Convention on Climate Change
(UNFCCC) 2
United Nations Human Settlements
Programme (UN-HABITAT) 19,
113, 160, 171–2
see also Habitat I; Habitat II;
Habitat III
United States 22, 25, 28, 43, 64,
92, 128
unrest, urban 63, 85
Unwin, Raymond 64
'urban accessibility pathways' 38, 46
'urban green commons' 84
urban sustainability 2–4, 7–8, 131,
145–59
and green cities 61, 62–3, 65, 72,
75, 90
weak and strong 7, 61, 72, 75,
153
Urbanafrica.net 172
urbanisation 1, 3, 5, 17, 18
and fair cities 112, 113, 120, 135
and green cities 62, 76, 151
urbanism, green 78
utopian thinking 7, 81, 110,
117–25, 151, 161, 162–3

V

value, economic 18, 78, 83, 150
value, qualitative 150–1
Vancouver, Canada **68**
village greens 63
villages, model 64
voluntarism 92, 93, 158
vulnerability 77

W

waste management xiv, 32, 69, 70,
86, 90
water supplies 42, 63, 69, 81, 87, 93,
126, 137n3
Waters, James 6–7, 29–48, 145, 148,
157
waterways 93
Weibull, J. 30

welfare 64, 110, 113, 115, 116, 123,
125, 126, 132
wellbeing 44, 148
and fair cities 108, 125
and green cities 62, 64, 65, 84
and urban density 23–4, 26,
29–30, 31
Welwyn Garden City 64
World Bank 12, 18, 28, 44, 134
World Conference on Environment
and Development (Rio de
Janeiro) 169
World Green Building Council
(WGBC) 168
Wright, Frank Lloyd 12, 66,
118–19, 124

Y

young people 63

Z

zoning 63, 157

Printed and bound by CPI Group (UK) Ltd, Croydon, CR0 4YY

13/04/2025

14656598-0001